A Maverick from Kansas

First Edition

Printed and bound in the United States of America

10 9 8 7 6 5 4 3 2 1

International Standard Book Number: 978-0-9851585-9-0
Library of Congress Control Number: 2021911207

Published by:
HERITAGE HISTORIES, LLC
1289 Fordham Blvd., Suite 271
Chapel Hill, North Carolina 27514
www.heritagehistories.com
919.616-5397

Dedication

I am dedicating these memories to my wonderful family, who all have contributed to my life in so many important ways that have overwhelmed me with gratitude and love for each and every one of them.

Table of Contents

California's Gifts

The little boy thought it all wondrous.

Not yet seven, Bob Medearis stood amid the crystalline fountains and dancing waters, gazed at the marble statues that seemed about to come to life, and strolled down the impossibly long espanades ringed by the colorful explosion of millions of flowers, and couldn't believe the spectacle. As he walked through the crowds with his parents and two older brothers, his head swiveled. The Golden Gate Exposition of 1939, themed the *Pageant of the Pacific* but which his parents called the San Francisco World's Fair, held more marvels than he could begin to comprehend.

Bob was old enough to know that the Depression had made life hard back home in Kansas City in recent years, though more so for others than his family, because Bob's father was a successful doctor. Money had still been tight since he could remember, though, so this family trip to the west coast had been a surprise. He could not have known that it would help set his course for life.

The drive had been long – several days in the family car – but when they finally rounded the bend on

the edge of Yerba Buena Island in San Francisco Bay, the
Exposition lay below them on Treasure Island like some
glittering Elysian city. As they passed along the causeway
on the western side of the island, Bob pressed his nose
against the side rear window and saw the Tower of the
Sun, a giant steeple stretching skyward from the middle of
the grounds and glistening with an ethereal whiteness in
the California sun against the bluest…and somehow
biggest… sky he had ever seen. Even the sun itself
seemed somehow brighter, more luminescent than the
one back in Kansas. Bob could not look away.

On the grounds he was stunned by the
magnificence of the buildings, the energy of the crowds,
even the complex fragrances spawned by the thousands
of varieties of flowers he could never have imagined. The
colorful murals, like that on the Federal Building, were so
unlike the dull gray edifices back home in downtown
Kansas City and the vast gardens so unlike the occasional
flowerbeds in his neighborhood as to make him think he
had entered another world. It all implied an abundance
and leisure that was in distinct contrast to their
comparatively dull and parsimonious life back home.

Bob particularly enjoyed the sea planes which set
out for the Far East from Clipper Cove, the small bay at
the south end of the island. Each China Clipper, as the
planes were called, looked like a great pregnant goose
sitting in the water with its wings outstretched atop the
fuselage and nose turned up on the bottom to brave the
waves. Once the smartly dressed crew had boarded, the
Clipper would motor slowly away from the pier to a point
well out in the Bay, then turn and throttle back toward
Treasure Island, building speed like an angry yacht with
wings. With roaring engines, the nose would lift out of

the air and seem to drag the rest of the plane with it. By the time the Clipper was back alongside Treasure Island, where it had started, it was a couple of hundred feet in the air; an instant later it would pass over the causeway to Yerba Buena and head for the Golden Gate. If Bob ran, he could cross the southwest corner of the Exposition to stand between the Egyptian-like ziggurats on the west side of the island facing San Francisco and watch the plane bisect the proud, red towers of the spectacular new Golden Gate Bridge in the distance like a football splitting the goal posts. Bob would continue to stare as the plane disappeared over the Pacific, a small emissary from civilization buzzing into the vastness of the ocean and heading to its first stop in Honolulu and eventually exotic, far-off Hong Kong.

As fascinating and glorious as they were, it wasn't the planes that fully stirred Bob's imagination. And it wasn't the Exposition's varied themes of exploration or the celebration of the many cultures that rimmed the Pacific. It was, in fact, the other features in this picture that kept the boy gazing long after the plane had taken off from the Cove or disappeared over the Pacific. It was the bridges.

Opened in 1936 and 1938, the Bay and Golden Gate Bridges were the reason for the Exposition, which featured the twin engineering feats to announce to the world the coming of age of the entire Bay Area as global community of the future.

Before he saw the Bay Bridge upon arriving from Kansas, of course, Bob saw the Bay itself. To a boy from Kansas, a bay was a small body of water, perhaps a jagged scallop nature had cut out of the shore of a lake. He always thought you could swim from shore to shore of a bay in a few minutes or throw a fishing line halfway across. Upon his first glimpse of the San Francisco Bay, though, he was gob smacked, speechless, and immediately thought it misnamed. This was not a bay, but a self-contained sea! He wondered how many fish swam in its great depths, thinking of the congenial little schools of bass, or catfish, or crappie that skittered about in the bays he knew back in Kansas and Missouri. There might even be sailfish in there!

It was the San Francisco Bay's magnitude that gave the bridges which spanned it their mystique. Bob associated the term "bridge" with the Hannibal Bridge in Kansas City, a piecemeal, blackened erector set of several large trusses spanning a relatively narrow section of the Missouri. The Bay Bridge arching over the massive San Francisco Bay – really a series of bridges, his father had explained – wasn't even in the same category, for it traversed miles…miles!...from Oakland to Yerba Buena Island, and then took to the air again to reach San Francisco, a two-part symphony in steel. Though he did not yet have the words for it…did not yet know the term "engineering" …Bob realized that there had to be some incredible type of building, or mechanical problem-solving for a bridge to span such incomprehensible distances. As they crossed it on their way to the Exposition and the roadway rose into the sky beneath them under the first suspension, Bob felt a small frisson of fear that was quickly subsumed under his fascination with the stanchions and the cables flying past the window. When he looked at it later from Treasure Island, the Bay Bridge seemed to be just like a spear from either side of Yerba Buena, its stanchions hung with swooping cables and creating, when viewed from a distance, an oscillating design against the sky which mirrored the waves pounding below. How, he wanted to know, had they done it?

He had the same visceral experience with the Golden Gate and the way it traversed its incredible chasm, and he was amazed not so much by the fact that it was the longest suspension bridge in the world, as his parents explained, but by the fact that they were so high above the water, and that the stanchions towered so high above the roadway. It was a colossus and, he knew, symbolic of the threshold between a burgeoning America and the mysteries of the East which lay beyond the vast Pacific Ocean. From the distance of Treasure Island, as he watched the China Clippers fly over it, the Golden Gate Bridge seemed almost a representation of the sunburned arms of Poseidon, stylized like the great statue of Pacifica at the Exposition, thrusting up and out of the water between San Francisco and Marin while holding a comparatively delicate ellipse of lace and plank between them. Again, young Bob wondered how it had been built.

And so began the little boy's fascination with bridges. Not fairs. Not planes. Not exploration. Bridges. That was one of two great gifts California gave Bob that summer of 1939, and they would start him on his life path.

The second gift California gave him was itself. Treasure Island was magical as an idea, but almost celestial in the reality. The streets lined with sculptures and gardens were nothing like Grandview Avenue, where he lived in Kansas City, the magnificent white buildings a dream compared to the dull edifices of his own downtown. And where Kansas City sat stolidly amidst

5

monotonous green and brown fields of wheat, Treasure Island floated like a jewel on a pristine, inland sea ringed on its watery horizons by hills and magical cities. Winter never came to California, he learned, only a refreshing coolness in the winter months, and fruit trees, warmed by the year-round sun, sprouted everywhere, even in people's yards. All Californians had to do was walk outside and pick something to eat anytime they wanted.

California was the closest place he could imagine to heaven on earth, and when this realization finally formed  in his mind, he turned to his parents and said, "Why would anyone leave here? I don't want to go home." It was, they thought, a common plea from a child on vacation, but the feeling never left Bob Medearis. From the first time he looked onto the San Francisco Bay as a small boy...from the moment he stood amid the wonders of Treasure Island, crossed the magnificent bridges and traversed the

My parents, Don and Gladys Medearis

enigmatic hills of San Francisco, California took root in his soul.

When the family left for home after that trip in 1939, Bob left with those two passions. The first, initially for bridges, was solidified as they headed back across the Bay Bridge, and the magic in its construction would once again not let him go. It would instead imbue him, as a parting gift, with deep questions about how things were built. Over time, Bob's fascination with the Bay and Golden Gate Bridges would foster other avenues of inquiry, and that curiosity would help forge from the wide-eyed little boy an engineer who would learn how bridges and many other things worked. Ultimately, he would set his hand to building things himself in a wide array of disciplines, but it was the newly built Bay and Golden Gate Bridges in 1939 which set him on his path into engineering.

The second passion was actually more of a deep longing. As the staccato rhythm of the bridge under the tires gave way to the road east, young Bob, his pleas about not wanting to go home more sincere and more powerful than his parents ever dreamed, peered sadly out the rear window until the last sparkle of sun on the waters of the Bay disappeared. He immediately began to wonder how he would slake his pining for California—the year-round sun, glistening cities, sparkling Bay and succulent, ever-present fruit that bent branches with their ripe weight. And somehow, he knew even then, as it disappeared behind him like a dream rinsed away by morning light, that California would forever be with him until he answered its call.

For the immediate future, Bob would return from his sun-drenched family vacation to a world that would, even thousands of miles and an ocean away, soon darken under the menacing shadows of an ominous world war. But over the next years, in the immediate day-to-day business of growing up, young Bob would go about his life sunnily embracing the pursuits of American boyhood: school and girls and sports and fishing in more manageable bays than the one in San Francisco.

Eventually, as he became a young man thinking more and more about his future, old dreams of the magical world out west he had visited years before would blink from the depths of his memory in ever-increasing intensity, like guiding stars that only emerge once the journey begins. And the twin gifts of a fascination with bridges and a longing for California, poignant and powerful invitations from his past, would alchemize first into a vague idea of building under an incessant sun, and eventually into a more crystallized vision around which, as he reached eighteen and Kansas began to shut its doors to him, he thought he might be able to build a life.

RWM

Roots

If there is any definitive truth about Bob Medearis as a young man, it is that he cut his own path. If he seemed destined for any profession, it would not have been engineering, but medicine. His grandfather and father were both physicians, and his older brother Don would be a celebrated physician as well. Generations back there were some farmers and merchants, and even some preachers, but there had been no engineers in the mix.

If he were to follow the family business, it would most likely be somewhere in the center of the country. As a multi-generation mid-westerner, California certainly had no claim on him: his paternal grandparents came from Illinois and Iowa and his maternal grandparents from Wisconsin, before they all moved to Kansas City, where both Bob's parents, and then Bob and his brothers, would grow up.

There was in fact nothing in young Bob's beginnings that would foreshadow the future he would eventually craft to the synaptic designs in his mind, like some decades-long, existential engineering project. On the other hand, over generations his family had fashioned a distinctly American story, the most distinctly American part being a penchant for finding and meeting opportunities wherever they may lie, even if far from home.

In that sense, Bob would follow suit from roots that reached far back in time.

My Father's Side
The Medearises (Portuguese Farmers)

Two hundred fifty miles due west of Morocco, floating alone in the blue Atlantic, sits a four-island archipelago, the largest island of which is a mountainous outpost known as Madeira where lush forests and exotic and colorful plants blanket the hills and waterfalls course off the highlands and into the sea. The entire four-island chain was mentioned in the first century by both Pliny the Younger and Plutarch as idyllic "purple islands",

The Island of Madeira
Courtesy of Frantishak

or the "Isles of the Blest", but the tiny archipelago wasn't officially "discovered" by the west until Henry the Navigator of Portugal set foot on the islands in the 15th century, claiming them for his motherland.

Immediate colonization followed, beginning in 1420, and when Portuguese and other Europeans planted wheat, grapes and sugar cane on the flatlands around the

Ciourtesy Mike Finn

perimeter of Madeira, slaves were imported from Africa and financiers in Genoa, seeking to bypass Venetian monopolies, financed a sugar mill. The grain failed in the sixteenth century, but western European traders continued to frequent the port in the main city of Funchal to stock up on Madeira wine and sugar.

This little speck in the Atlantic, which produced the wine which Thomas Jefferson and the Continental Congress used to toast U.S. independence, is the ancestral home of the Medearises, and the place where our name originated.

The first Medearis known to history, my eighth great-grandfather, was Caledonia Medearis, born in 1537. (His father's name has been lost.)[1] Caledonia's son, Pedro, was born in 1570, and his grandson, Domingo, my sixth great-grandfather, was born in 1620. In 1617, three years before Domingo was born,

Madeira Wine

North African pirates captured 1,200 people in Porto Santo, an island in the archipelago just a few kilometers northeast of Madeira. That may have been what provided the impetus for Pedro to emigrate, when he came of age,

---

[1] In the sixteenth through eighteenth centuries, the name is spelled Medearis, Maderas, Medaris, and even Madrigal. For the purposes of simplicity we are sticking with the modern spelling throughout.

to the New World. He settled in what today is Middlesex County in eastern Virginia between the Dragon Swamp and the Rappahannock River.

It is clear that the Medearises were a wealthy family in Madeira, almost certainly planters of sugar cane or grapes, for Domingo had the means before leaving the island to sponsor many other people to come to the New World, thereby earning headrights, which provided him 50 acres of land in America for each individual he sponsored. Many of these people in turn served Domingo for a number of years as indentured servants to pay off their debt. In addition to the extensive property by the Dragon Swamp, where Domingo lived, ranched, and farmed tobacco, he also owned 1,500 acres elsewhere in Virginia. Farmers in the Dragon Swamp area like Domingo Medearis used a sweetly scented Spanish tobacco originally imported from Barbados, and it was the backbone of the economy in this region. The farmers there used a unique method, taught them by native Americans, of planting small mounds into which a single tobacco plant was placed.

Domingo's home was likely typical for a 17th century Virginia farmer: a simple wooden cabin with a dirt floor and a large interior room dominated by a massive stone fireplace for cooking. There was probably a loft or attic for supplies and for the children's sleeping area. Small wooden sheds for drying the tobacco leaves would have been clustered about the property, all of which was likely surrounded by a picket fence. Paths led between houses and farms and to the Rappahannock River about a half mile northeast.

The next three generations of Medearises – Carlos Charles, born in 1665, John Thomas, born in 1703, and

Oliver, my third great-grandfather, born in 1759, grew up by the Dragon Swamp and were likely farmers like Domingo. In 1782 Oliver married Wilmuth Redmund of Chatham, Virginia, not far from the North Carolina border, and they had most of their nine children, including Abraham, born in 1787, in Guilford County, North Carolina.

Abe Medearis's Land Record

When the first U.S. census was taken in 1790, Oliver and Wilmuth lived in Guilford County just southwest of Wilmuth's family home in Chatham, Virginia, and where Oliver owned about 300 acres along Troublesome Creek, next to his brother Charles and northwest of present-day Greensboro. There is some record of Oliver fighting in the Revolution through pay accounts for North Carolina regiments, and through the fact that he was, like many veterans of the Revolutionary War, given land as a reward for his service. Oliver's land grant was in "Union Township" just east of Cincinnati, Ohio, and so around 1804, he and Wilmuth and their family moved with about 50 other families to Ohio. Because of frequent Indian attacks on the way, women usually went by flatboats on the river, while men traveled nearby by wagon train.

Oliver and Wilmuth lived in the Union Township area of Ohio for 25 years, before moving late in life, likely to be near Abraham, who had moved to Shelby County, near Sidney, in the central part of the state. In his will, Oliver wrote, "I will and bequeath to my loving wife Wilmoth Medearis the one third part of all my Estate Real and Personal During her widowhood for her maintenance for as long as she lives." He gave, "one Dollar each after my Decease to wit to my son Abraham Medearis my daughters Newlilly Lucas Regina Stuart and Sally Davis...I further will and bequeath my land to be sold after my wife's Death and equally divided among all my heirs with all other property that may be remaining after her death." Oliver died in 1829, and is buried in Pioneer Cemetery in Plattsville, in southeast Shelby County.

After moving with his parents to Ohio, Abraham married Charity Catherine Ellsworth in 1814 in Champaign County, Ohio. In 1827, Abraham purchased nearby land, "between the Miami and Little Miami Rivers" according to land records in Cincinnati. This was likely the family's first foothold in Shelby County, which was just to the west of his wife's family home in Champaign. After his father's death, Abraham's mother Wilmuth lived with him until she died on 19 May 1842 and was buried in Pioneer Cemetery next to Oliver.

Abraham and Charity had eight children, the ninth of which was Thomas Beecher Medearis, my great-grandfather, who was born in Shelby County in 1826. In 1860, Thomas married Mary Helen Ingersoll, who had been born in 1835 in Cuyahoga, Ohio, near Cleveland. As a young couple, Thomas and Helen moved to Mound Township in McDonough County in Illinois, about halfway between Chicago and St. Louis, where he could farm. Thomas fought in an Illinois regiment during the Civil War, though records are scanty.

When Thomas's father, Abraham, got cancer about 1850, he and Charity moved from Ohio to Illinois to live with Thomas. After Abraham died in Thomas's home four days after Christmas in 1859, Charity moved to Gardner Township, Kansas, to live with her daughter, Thomas's sister, Wilmoth, who was living there with her husband James Vanice.

In 1910, Thomas and Helen, now aged themselves, moved to be near their son, Reuben, in Gravette, Arkansas, and about 1916 they actually moved into his house. Mary, known as Grandma Medearis, died in 1917 in Gravette after breaking her hip in a fall. "Mrs. Medearis was a good and true wife," according to her obituary in the *Gravette News-Herald*, "a kind and thoughtful mother, ever ready to help the poor, the sick and needy in her younger life." Thomas died two years later, in 1919. "He had been quite feeble for some months," wrote the *News-Herald*. Thomas and Mary's son, Reuben's brother, Dr.

My paternal grandparents, Charles Marcellus and Abigail Medearis, with my father, Don

Charles Marcellus Medearis of Kansas City, was reported in the paper to have attended the funerals.

Charles Medearis was my grandfather. He was born in Mound Township, Illinois, in January of 1861 to Thomas and Mary. His son (my father) Dr. Donald N. Medearis, wrote in his autobiography that "after a boyhood spent on the farm, [Charles] had brief careers as a schoolteacher and as a surveyor in western Kansas before beginning the study of medicine in the old Northwestern Medical School of St. Joseph,

Missouri. My father began his practice of medicine in Kansas City, Kansas, and continued in this profession until his death in 1977."

Charles married my grandmother, Abigail Norman in Logan, Iowa, in 1895, where her parents, Alfred and Lucinda Norman, had moved from Illinois. Charles and Abby had two children together, my father Donald, born in 1901 and my aunt Clara, who died around the age of ten in 1905. After Abigail died 1919 at age 53, my grandfather remarried Maude Engle Cole in Missouri. *[It appears from marriage records and census data that Charlie and Abby jumped the gun a bit, as Clara was born in August 1895, a month before her parents were married in Logan, Iowa, but we can leave that out.]*

The Normans (Englishmen and Soldiers)

My grandmother, Abigail was born in Illinois Abigail Rosella Norman to Alfred and Lucinda Norman.

The first Norman was actually Robert, my eighth great-grandfather, who was born in Netherbury, Dorset, England in 1663, in southwest England. Netherbury is a village nestled in beautiful valley through which rolls the River Brit. The village sits about seven miles north of England's spectacular and rocky Jurassic Coast, a set of cliffs scalloped out of England's southwestern-most peninsula. About a hundred years and four generations later, Robert's great-grandson, John Peter Norman, was born in 1735, 130 miles west of Netherbury on the River Camel in the fishing village Padstow, Cornwall, England, on the north coast of the same peninsula. John Peter was the Norman who came to the U.S., first to Warwick, New York, north of New York City and west of the Hudson

River, before moving west to the Sparta, New Jersey area. Peter, as he was known, died in 1795 in Monmouth, New Jersey, at the age of 60.

Peter's son Oliver, my fourth great-grandfather, born in 1763, moved from New York to Muskingum, Ohio, in the west central part of the state. The next several generations – Thomas, born in 1789; Joseph, born in 1814; and Alfred, born in Logansport, Indiana, 1837, moved steadily west. In 1859, Alfred married Lucinda Colton in Mason County, Illinois, just 15 miles from where Charles Medearis was living with his family in Mound Township.

During the Civil War, Alfred enlisted in Company E of the Illinois 86th Infantry Regiment. In 1862, Company E marched to Washington, D.C., via Richmond, Virginia, April 29-May 19, 1865, and mustered out June 6, but there is some question about whether he was still in the regiment at this time. Well after the war, Alfred and Lucinda moved a couple of hundred miles north to Lasalle, Illinois, and then later to Logan, Iowa, 30 miles due north of Omaha.

Lucinda gave birth to Abigail, my grandmother, in August of 1865. In his autobiography, my father writes that his mother "was also of an Illinois farm family, moved to Logan, Iowa, with the family, graduated at Highland Park College in Des Moines, and was a schoolteacher before marrying my grandfather."

Curiously Abigail and Charles lived near each other a couple of times in their early years, the first being when both lived as small children within a few miles of Mason, Illinois, and the second 15 years later in Logan, Iowa, in 1880, where Abby was in high school, before heading off to college, and 18-year-old Charles was listed as a farmer.

Wherever and however they met, Abigail Rosella Norman and Charles Marcellus Medearis married in Logan in 1895 and eventually moved to Kansas City where Charles was a physician. Abigail gave birth to my father, Donald N. Medearis in Kansas City in 1902.

My Mother's Side
The Sandfords (English Woolen Magnates)

My mother was born Gladys Sandford in 1903 in Kansas City to Walter S. and Jessie Leville Sandford. Her entire family was Scottish and English.

The first Sandford of whom we know, William, my fourth great- grandfather, was born in 1786 in Huddersfield, Yorkshire, England in the English midlands between Liverpool and Leeds, where he spent his life. Huddersfield, recorded in the *Domesday Book* of 1086 as "Oderesfel", is the site of two forts, one dating from the Iron Age and another from Roman times. Huddersfield has been a market town since Anglo-Saxon times, and the ancient market cross is still in the marketplace.

In the fourteenth century, the local manor was the property of the de Lacy family, but reverted to royal ownership in 1322. In 1599 it fell into the hands of the Ramsden family who owned it until the early twentieth century. They supported the textile industry, building the Cloth Hall, a center for textile trading, and the Sir John Ramsden's Canal in 1780, which provided transportation for local manufacturers and merchants to move their product.

William's son, Joseph, born in 1786, and grandson Samuel, born in 1807, both lived in Yorkshire. Elysium, the Sandford family home built around the time of Samuel's birth, still stands at Cartworth near Holmfirth. In 1830 Samuel married Emalia Haigh at All Hallows Parish Church in Kirkburton, Yorkshire, and together they had twelve children, three of whom died in infancy. Like many in the area, Sandford was a woolen manufacturer. In 1856 he inherited an estate from an uncle, where he lived for 13 years, before selling it and retiring to a cottage home.

In May of 1869, Samuel - but not Amelia -- and his grown son Jonathan and Jonathan's wife, Malinda, emigrated to Wisconsin. Samuel then returned to England and he and Amelia returned to the U.S. on the *City of Paris*, sailing from Liverpool and arriving in New York on July 31, 1871.

In the interim, Jonathan, Malinda and their son Walter, born in 1870 in Wisconsin, had moved to a farm in Morris County, Kansas, about 140 miles west of Kansas City, so Samuel and Amelia traveled there to be with family. Unfortunately, the trip may have proved too much for Amelia as she passed away in Kansas before the end of the year.

Eight years later, in 1879, Samuel returned for one year to England, then came back to Kansas, where he died at age 77 in Morris County in 1883. His obituary noted his "strong traits of character and honesty." He was also said to "have worn a silk top hat and spats."

Jonathan and Malinda's son, Walter, my grandfather, married Jessie Leville Garner in 1900. They moved to Kansas City where Walter was a postal clerk with the railroad, mostly likely the iconic Atchison, Topeka & Santa Fe Railway, which had been chartered in 1859. Kansas and the Midwest were veined with railroads, but the Atchison ran through Parkerville, in Morris County, where Walter grew up, and it's likely he found the job there. Postal clerks with the railroad were common in the nineteenth century because railway post offices, or RPOs, were railroad cars designated solely for mail on passenger trains. The postal clerks who managed the RPOs were highly trained, and mail delivery was often more lucrative than passenger traffic for the railroads at the time.

While the Sandfords are only traceable back to 1746, it is through my great-great-grandmother Amelia Haigh Sandford, who passed away after accompanying her husband Samuel Sandford from Yorkshire to the wheat fields of Kansas in 1871, that our family is traceable most deeply into the mists of ancient history. The first Haigh of which we know, Edmund, was born in 1590 in Bradshaw Almondbury Parish in Yorkshire, and was my 11th great grandfather. Almondbury Parish was a couple of miles southeast of Huddersfield, also part of the de Lacy holdings, and also the site of an important market in the Middle Ages. The line from Edmund to Amelia 200 years later is uninterrupted, and entirely in Yorkshire.

The Garners (Scottish Flax Merchants)

My maternal grandmother, Jessie Leville Garner, was born in Morris County, Kansas, in 1881, and married my grandfather, Walter Sandford, there in 1900.

The Garners were Scottish, reaching back to Gavin Garner, my fifth great-grandfather, who was born in New Monkland, Lanarkshire, Scotland in 1691 and married Agnes Baillie in 1730. Lanarkshire is a region in the rolling Scottish midlands, southeast of Glasgow and southwest of Edinburgh by about 30 miles each. The area's dry, clay soil lent itself to the growing of flax, a plant used in the making of linseed oil and coarse fabrics, and which naturally became a primary crop and industry of the area until it was overtaken by cotton a century later.

Gavin's grandson, Thomas Garner, my third great-grandfather, was born in New Monkland in 1754, and was listed as a "flax grower." Some records also list

The Garners, John Garner, second from left and his sons George, Thomas and Robert Garner, shortly before John's death in 1895

him as a flax grower in Ireland, so there is strong evidence he emigrated there before moving on to the U.S., where he settled originally in New Jersey. After a life in New Jersey, Thomas died in 1836 in White Lake, Michigan, a suburb of Detroit in the Oakland area, where he likely moved in his dotage to live with his son John.

John Garner, my great-great grandfather was born in Hardiston, Sussex, New Jersey, in 1805 and moved to White Lake, where he married a woman named Christina Bachman, and farmed until his death in 1895.

John's son William, my great-grandfather, was born in White Lake in 1843. In 1861, shortly after the Civil War broke out, William enlisted in the First Regiment, United States Lancers, Michigan, which was organized by Colonel Arthur Rankin in the winter of 1860-61 in various Michigan cities, including Detroit. The Lancers were mustered out on March 20, 1862, without seeing active service.

John and Sarah (second wife) and Garner's homestead on White Lake rail in Michigan

Garner then joined the Michigan Light Artillery which was organized in March of 1862 – the same month the First Regiment mustered out. The Artillery was composed of twelve, six-gun batteries and was commanded by Colonel L.C. Loomis. About a hundred men were scattered through these batteries, A, C, D, G, H, I, L and M, although they were never brought together as a full regiment.

William Garner was in Battery H, which rendezvoused in March of 1862 in Monroe, Michigan, under the command of Captain Samuel DeGobyer and immediately reported to General Halleck at St. Louis. Thence Battery H was ordered to New Madrid, Missouri, and afterward served in Kentucky, west Tennessee and northern Mississippi, taking an active part in the Mississippi campaign which preceded the siege of Vicksburg. The operations of Battery H were conducted entirely in Mississippi and Georgia, its last engagement being at Lovejoy's Station, Georgia, in August of 1864.

Civil War veteran William Garner, my great-grandfather

Family lore says Garner was slightly injured at the battle of Gettysburg, but Battery H was at the Battle of Vicksburg at the time, so he may have been there. Or he could have been in Battery I, which marched across Virginia to Washington and then saw action at Gettysburg.

Assuming he stayed with H, after going down the Mississippi with Grant, which is what Battery H did, the story goes that, as the war wound down, William was assigned over to Sherman, and joined in the march through Georgia in the fall of 1864 when Sherman burned everything in sight. If William did not return to Michigan from Lovejoy's Station in Georgia, Battery H's last battle, this is highly probable, for he could very well have joined General Kilpatrick's Army, which Sherman had sent as reinforcements to Lovejoy's Station, and which subsequently joined back up with Sherman for the march through Atlanta and the Carolinas in November and December of 1864.

Later in life, Garner reported at being outraged, as a farmer himself, that Sherman was burning farms to the ground and laying waste to the countryside. When he deserted, disgusted at Sherman's actions, Sherman wanted to give him a dishonorable discharge, but according to

Garner, Grant intervened and said that Garner had been one of his best soldiers and had even been given four battlefield commissions.

Indeed, the record shows Garner was promoted, while in Battery H of the Light Cavalry, from private to Full Corporal on 15 Oct 1862; to Full Sergeant on 23 Apr 1863; to Full 1st Lieutenant on 29 May 1865; and to Full 2nd Lieutenant on 01 Jan 1865. This also suggests he remained with Battery H and was at Vicksburg rather than Gettysburg.

Grant insisted that Sherman give William an honorable discharge, and he finally mustered out in August of 1865 at Jackson, Michigan, with a stipend of 60 acres in Morris County, Kansas, where he moved to farm after the war.

When people asked William later why he left his farm in Michigan for Kansas, Garner's response was that a lot of soldiers would be getting 60 acres, as he had, and since many of them didn't know how to farm, they would be willing to part with it…which is how Garner ended up with vast amounts of Kansas farmland.

Garner married Ellen Crittenden of New York, and after the war, their daughter, Jessie Leville was born in Morris County in 1881. Jessie met and in 1900 married the son of another Morris County farmer, Walter Sandford. They moved to Kansas City, where my mother Gladys was born in 1903.

Without Ulysses Grant's intervention, Lieutenant William Garner would likely have received a dishonorable discharge without a stipend in Kansas, and simply moved back to Michigan. His daughter Jessie would have never met Walter Sandford, my mother would have never been born…and none of us would be here!

In truth, Ulysses Grant was but the last of a thousand random circumstances which led to people in the Medearis, Norman, Sandford and Garner clans meeting and marrying through history. But that is the story of any family. Ours began centuries ago on the little island of Madeira and in the rolling hills of Scotland and England, and after crossing the Atlantic in the nineteenth century took root in the twentieth in the heartland of America, from where I continued the journey west to California. My daughter Ilsi has built a life there, on the west coast, but my sons Dale and Ken are the first in a dozen generations to turn the tide and head east, raising their families back in Washington D.C.

RWM

Chapter Two:
A Kansan Looking West
1932-50

I was born on the 18th of May 1932.

At the time the U.S. and the world were in the depths of the Depression. The stock market had crashed two-and-a-half years before, in October of 1929, and people were wiped out in an instant. Stockbrokers in New York, overextended by buying on margins that were later outlawed, jumped out of windows. Businesses closed, jobs were lost, and homeless people in cities like Kansas City formed shantytowns called Hoovervilles, named after Herbert Hoover, the president on whose watch the Depression began. Breadlines – long lines of people waiting for free food handed out by private charities like the Red Cross – snaked around gray city corners as children in large families took turns eating on alternate days.

The year I was born Franklin Roosevelt won the presidency and immediately initiated the New Deal, a host of government programs generating work for the one quarter of the workforce which had no job, and the rest who were underemployed. Many public buildings, bridges, dams, and other projects still around today were New Deal projects.

Kansas City was no different than any other American city, and the rest of the state was suffering the effects of a massive drought which turned the Midwest into what became known as the Dust Bowl. Great billowing clouds of dust would mushroom up from the desiccated earth and sweep across the devastated crops and into cities, blackening the sky and driving people inside so they could breathe.

Our family was fortunate because my father was a physician, but we were not wealthy. He sometimes took vegetables, milk and eggs in payment for his services so he could continue to provide medical care to those who could no longer afford it. We didn't have a lot of extras, but we didn't miss any meals either.

Our family's home on Grandview in Kansas City, where I grew up, is still there today.

When I was born, the third of three brothers, the older two being Don, five years my senior and Ken, almost three years older, we lived on Greeley Avenue, west of Kansas City, Kansas downtown. I don't remember that house very well, other than we had a long narrow backyard that ran up against a railroad track, a spur which served a small shuttle carrying coal, as I remember it, to the power company.

We soon moved a few miles southeast, closer to the Kansas River, to 2200 Grandview Boulevard. This was a couple of miles west of Kansas City, Kansas – across the Kansas River and the West Bottoms – from downtown Kansas City, Missouri. Our house was a two-story, white frame house on the corner of 22nd Street, very near where Central Avenue, a major thoroughfare which ran from Kansas City, Missouri, to the northwest part of Kansas City, Kansas, cut diagonally across Grandview.

That's the house that I was raised in until I went away to college. It has been redone several times over the years, and the huge elm trees have all been cut down now. My parents lived there until I was at Stanford in the early 1950s, and Dad was starting the retirement process.

Chores

All three of us kids were given chores. Everybody was responsible for certain thing., but I gravitated into gardening. I guess that came from my interest in the farm the Sandford family had, as well as other relatives like the Blythes (my grandmother's younger sister) that were in the business. I raised a lot of beans and other vegetables, particularly during the war years. I just loved it.

I greatly admired my older brother Ken. He was the social animal in our house. We shared a bed until I was five or six, which was the tradition at that time. I was the little kid, but we were very good friends, and had a very close relationship.

I didn't know too much about Don, because he was so much older, but I knew my folks worried about him a lot. Then as now, parents tend to worry about the first child.

I walked to all the schools I attended – Park Grade School, Central Junior High School for sixth and seventh, and finally, Wyandotte High School. We had a choice of taking eighth grade at junior high or high school, and my brothers went to Central Junior High for three years, but I didn't like the long walk in the winter and Wyandotte was closer, so I went into high school for my freshman year after two years at Central.

Though we walked to school we travelled around town by streetcar. There were hundreds running on the tracks down the middle of streets all over town. They ran until the 1950s. We paid by tokens that we bought and put in the canister at the front, like a bus today. I think it was unlimited mileage for a nickel. There were no restrictions on the three

A streetcar like the ones we used to ride when I was a boy

Medearis boys…we just had check in when we got home. It wasn't like today…everybody looked out for everybody.

One of the things we have lost in this country is the sense of self organization and structure…kids just playing on their own, getting up or making up games on the fly. We had a group we ran with, and so sometimes we'd play basketball at the goal my parents put up in the backyard, because I really wanted to be able to play at the house. Usually though, we'd go to the park across the street from our house. It's still there. It's triangular in shape, and there were rocks and bushes and trees. We played hide and seek, king of the mountain, all of that. It was self-structured. Sometimes we turned it all into a baseball diamond. We laid out what the paths were...first base was the stone over on the right next to the bank, we moved a flat stone to be second base, and then over right next to the sidewalk was third...things like that. Everybody agreed and there was no argument because all of us kids made the rules. We were all disciplined and we all followed our own rules.

Of course, we didn't think about it then, but in hindsight it was really a beautiful thing to watch. We've lost that...the sense of creativity and improvisation and independence. Today the parents, or organized sports, structure everything. Kids don't design their own play anymore.

Roger Buford, our next-door neighbor, was in our crowd. Roger's father bought and sold wheat, but he was also a baker, and I well remember him making bread and then making peanut butter sandwiches for us...they were absolutely the best peanut butter and jelly sandwiches I've ever eaten in my life. I don't know what was so special about that bread and homemade peanut butter. Those were just marvelous days.

War Years

When the war broke out in '41 it was a real jolt. I was nine. My brother Don was about 15, and Ken was around 13, so throughout the entire war I was very young – between ten and fourteen, in junior high school.

The war had been raging in Europe for a couple of years, but it really started for the United States on

December 7, 1941, when the Japanese bombed Pearl
Harbor. That Sunday we had gone to church – we went
to London Heights Methodist – and then went to our
grandparents', Grandma and Grandpa Sandford, for
Sunday dinner. They didn't live too far away, in a white,
three-bedroom brick and frame house, like ours, sitting
on a bluff. I remember they had a cellar with a washboard
and big wash pans that had all the laundry in them.

My grandfather had been a schoolteacher, but he
didn't make enough money doing that, so he had left to
become a railroad postal clerk. He was a postal clerk
when I was very young, but he retired during the war.

Sunday dinner at my grandparents usually involved
fried chicken, hot buttered peas, mashed potatoes and
gravy and a salad, and then chocolate cake and ice cream
for dessert. That Sunday was different, because about
noon Franklin Roosevelt came on the radio to say Pearl
Harbor had been struck. The news spread like wildfire
and all across the country people turned their radios on
and were listening throughout the day.

I remember it was all very somber...very, very
serious. Everybody was scared to death. The animosity in
that part of the country had been, until that day, directed
towards the Germans, because the war in Europe had
been between our allies, England and France. By that
time, we had some Hispanics, Irish, Polish in Kansas City
– no Asians yet – but there were a lot of people with
German ancestry and a lot of German influence. As an
example of anti-German sentiment, I can remember we
had once gone up to Cincinnati, and had dinner at
Mecklenburg Gardens, which was a landmark local
German restaurant and beer garden. But with the war, no

one was about to honor a German restaurant. People felt that way all over the country.

My father was very patriotic and right away he wanted to sign up. The Army wouldn't accept him, despite the fact that he was a runner, because of his very severe arthritis. I can remember him crying all night long, not being able to go off to war to serve his country. I felt very sorry for Dad not getting in.

The country was really ramped up during the war years. We learned about propaganda and witnessed victory gardens sprout in front yards and saw war posters go up on walls. Lots of little idiosyncrasies like this came with the war. At the very beginning, soldiers marched down State Avenue next to our high school in Kansas City. I can remember these parades and songs like *Roll Out the Barrel, We'll Have a Barrel of Fun, Boogie Woogie Bugle Boy,* and of course, *Stars and Stripes Forever.*

Television was developed in the mid-1940s, and that became the main communication vehicle of the government to the people, but actual live war coverage didn't begin until 25 years later, during Vietnam. I clearly remember Roosevelt's radio "fireside chats," which were evening radio addresses he started during the Depression to encourage and reassure people. These continued throughout World War II. My father didn't like them at all because he didn't like Roosevelt.

Things changed at school too. There were collections for aluminum and for special causes, like funds for battlefield injuries. There was a national passion for supporting the troops. One big change was the rationing of commodities like gasoline. Dad was quite worried about whether he would have enough gasoline to make house calls (which doctors regularly did in those days!). It turned out he didn't; the rationing was so severe that he had to have the people come to him on the streetcars. Gas rationing altered the practice of medicine significantly.

Fort Riley was not too far from Kansas City, and we would always have soldiers visit at Thanksgiving and Christmas. As kids we were really tied into that. It brought the reality of the war home to us to have soldiers at the house. We had some of those guys back several years later, or they'd stop by the house when they were back in town. We developed some wonderful relationships that way.

The jobs I had during that period were interesting. There were always a lot of collections for the war effort, but being the youngest of three, I was sheltered, and a lot of what I did was determined by what my brothers were doing. I can remember going over to the city park and riding in the jeeps for $25 which bought a war bond. We also worked harvest on the family farms. I did that for two summers.

As we entertained soldiers and watched parades and collected things for the war effort and underwent rationing, news about the war would dribble in slowly. It wasn't like today, and it's hard to imagine, but the news would only come in days after the fact. I remember that we got the news early on, the first part of 1942, about the battles at Guadalcanal and Midway. These were both Allied victories over the Japanese in the Pacific and cause for great hope and celebration, but the war would go on for three more years.

We had a cousin, John Blythe, who set the standard for everybody during the very early stages of the war. John was 10 or 15 years older than me, and lived on his family's farm in White City, Kansas. We were very close to him. He wanted to fly, but the U.S. didn't have an Air Force – we had an Army Air Force but there wasn't a U.S. Air Force – so early on he went to Canada to join the Canadian Air Force and learn how to fly Spitfires. The Canadians were activated by the Brits during the Battle of Britain, and John flew Spitfires in defense of England.

Later, U.S. General "Hap" Arnold, who was soon-to-be commanding general of the U.S. Army Air Force, announced that anybody who had flown for England was welcome to bring their Spitfires and crews and join the American forces going into North Africa. So John flew in North Africa, Sicily and Italy before they discharged him. I really resonated with him when I was a little older and he came back after the war.

Of course, as time went on, my older brother Don reached 18 and was drafted. That hit home pretty hard. After graduating from high school, he went to hospital training camp in Great Lakes. In late summer of 1945, he was on a boat going to Okinawa to be in the first wave of a major invasion to land in Japan. It was always felt that the first wave was the death wave, so all those guys were facing great peril when Harry Truman dropped the bomb. That was August 6, 1945, and that probably saved Don and everyone else on those ships. No doubt about it. Truman was actually a pretty good president.

We knew the war was winding down in June of '44 when news came back about D- Day, and how we routed the Germans on the beaches of Normandy. After that it was pretty clear sailing.

The war years were really a very traumatic time, but you didn't think about death. I learned later about some of the horrors of that war by hearing about what my wife Helga's side of the family went through. I read story after story on that. War is such a stupid thing. It is the height of man's inhumanity towards men. There's no good to it whatsoever.

Uncle Dale

There was one other sad and traumatic thing that happened when I was little, and this occurred well before the war, in 1936.

Uncle Dale Sandford was my mother's brother. He was an officer in the Army, and in 1936, when I was a little over four years old, he arranged for me to go up in a biplane, which was my first airplane ride. He also gave me my first motorcycle ride. I credit him with really expanding my horizons.

In April of that year, 1936, Uncle Dale was murdered. I remember it all. I remember Mom crying so much.

The official line was that a man named Raymond Boyer had met Dale in a tavern in Kansas City, and then took him hostage for his car. Boyer drove across the intercity viaduct – the old national highway 40 – and made his way toward St. Louis, and seven hours later shot Dale near Oak Grove, Missouri. He told police that he had decided to tie Dale up, then saw Dale had a gun and shot him.

My older brother Don and I talked about this a lot later, and are not sure this is what actually happened, despite it being the "official story." We came to the conclusion that there was something more personal involved...that they knew each other somehow and that

Dale was shot as a result of an argument or grudge. The whole hostage thing didn't really seem to add up to us. In any case, Boyer was apprehended, convicted, tried and executed in thirty days. Justice is swift in Kansas.

My father said, "I want you to learn something from this. What I want you to learn is that the state had no right to take that man's life, because when they did that, they became murderers just like the guy they were prosecuting." I've never, ever forgotten that, and from that moment I've never believed in capital punishment.

My Father

Most people end up modeling a few of the characteristics of their folks, sometimes to a great extent. Or they become the opposite. In our house, we really revered Dad, or at least Ken and I did. We pretty much put him on a pedestal. I really don't know where Don was on that. He was more aloof.

For Ken, and I don't know if he would agree with this, I think he probably had a better relationship with our mother. For me, my father was the biggest influence on my life, and I loved him. He was a busy man but that was not an issue; we had a great relationship.

One thing that defined him was his brilliance. He was a very, very bright man. He went through the University of Kansas with straight A's and then to Harvard Medical School. Don inherited Dad's brilliance. More important than Dad's intelligence, though, was his integrity, his honesty. I always admired that about him and aspired to meet his standard.

Dad did not like people who worked on the backs of others. That's the best way I can describe his political outlook. We talked a lot about that. He couldn't stand Roosevelt – he thought he was a demagogue. He didn't like Truman at first just because he was Democrat. He changed his mind when Truman took over the presidency and turned out to be a very good president, particularly after he dropped the bombs and ended the war.

Dad had very staunch Midwestern values, but I don't think he got them from his father. In the Midwest generally there was strong loyalty to service model...it was driven into every family I knew. My father's values absolutely got through to me. Unfortunately, I don't think these values have been adequately passed on to the following generations, which I think is a tragedy.

I remember one unusual thing that occurred surrounding his being a doctor and how he would handle sickness in the family. If one kid caught the measles, then Dad would place us all under a tent and we would have to breathe each other's air. He figured we would all get it anyway, so he wanted us all to be sick at the same time, so he could treat us at the same time. It was pretty unusual for a pediatrician to do that.

Pediatricians just didn't make that much money, and Dad really didn't make good money until the end of the 1950's or the early 1960's. He didn't care about money, though. He really cared about service. That just was driven into everything that man did. It is a remarkable thing to have. He was a huge, huge factor in that way, on my later career.

My Grandfathers

I did not know Dad's father, also Dr. Medearis, that well. He died when I was very young. The only thing

I can remember about my grandfather Medearis was that he loved rice. He had a bowl of rice every morning for his breakfast...rice, milk and cinnamon. I eat that a lot myself. I switched more to granola than rice, but I like that.

I had a terrific relationship with my grandfather Sandford. I really enjoyed being with my grandfather. I guess partly because he'd been an English teacher, as he was smart and well-read. He was a prolific novel reader and read all the current stuff...magazines and newspapers. He read lots of books to me.

He was very kind, very much the loving, active, caring grandfather. My grandmother was a little bit more reserved, but similar in demeanor. Very often Ken would be with Mom, Don would be with Dad, and I would be with Grandpa. That's just the way life is...you gravitate towards things of mutual interest. For instance, I don't think my brothers wanted to learn about fly fishing the way I did. But Grandpa and I went fishing a lot together in his '36 Ford. That was a great automobile! I became a pretty good fly fisherman and have fished all over the continent...Canada and Alaska. Mainly we fished and did a lot of reading.

One time, grandfather Medearis turned a summer scout camp disaster into a great fishing experience. My parents wanted us all to be in scouts, but we didn't have a very good scout group. That's ironic, as I'm a very proud father of two Eagle Scouts. I didn't do as well as a scout as my boys, though. My highest rank was Star Scout, but I couldn't stand the local scouts or the scout troop. It was a loose knit organization and the hikes in Kansas were boring and dull. Here in California Ken and Dale hiked the Sierras...it was just so much different. Helga and I both participated. Helga has been on more fifty milers than most scouts. We didn't have the Sierras in Kansas, of course, which is a great incentive to be outdoors.

One summer when I was about twelve or thirteen my parents sent me to Camp Philmont, the Boy Scout camp in New Mexico. My family put me on the train for New Mexico at Union Station in Kansas City, Missouri, and then the whole family except for me took off for their own trip to Yellowstone.

Philmont was a day-and-a-half ride across two full states. It was a long trip. When I got there, they said the camp was closed because of an infantile paralysis outbreak, and they gave me a ticket to go back home. I knew there was nobody there, but I decided I might as well enjoy the train ride back and see what happens. What else could I do?

When I got home, I called Grandpa and Grandma and I told them what had happened, and said, "I'm here at the train station. What are you doing for the next two weeks? I'm here and Mom and Dad are gone." There was no way to reach Mom and Dad, or at least it didn't make any sense to try.

Grandpa said, "Terrific. I'm glad you caught me here. Stay right there at the train station and I'll pick you up in one hour, because I need to grab the fishing poles and some food. We're going to go fly fishing for a couple of weeks in Minnesota and Canada." So we drove up to Canada and fly fished for a couple of weeks. That was a lot better than Camp Philmont! A disaster turned into ideal vacation for this young man.

Five years later, when I was about 18, a close friend named Allen Ditzen and I went on the same trip over the summer. Allen had gone in the service as a pilot, but he had taken a leave, so we went up fly fishing in Canada in my grandfather's same '36 Ford. I loved that car. At the last minute my grandfather threw in a cow hide. He said, "I don't know what you're going to do with this," he said, "but it might come in handy. Keep your mind open." So we got up there just north of Duluth, and we were burning oil. That's when I realized what that cow hide was for. We took the broken gasket off the manifold and replaced it with the cowhide, which lasted for 4,000 miles before we had to change it.

We had sleeping bags and slept in the car or in the open air outside. When we got up to fishing and we were north of Minnesota, in Canada, Lake of the Woods. That was a great two weeks, and I thought Grandpa was a genius. He saved our trip with his cow hide. He was alive at that point but died later when I was on my way out to Stanford. Sadly, Allen Ditzen, my best Kansas buddy, was killed in Korea. His death had a profound effect on me as I missed him greatly.

Other Influences

My second-grade schoolteacher at Park Elementary School, Mrs. Simms, was a great teacher and a huge disciplinarian. She had a huge impact on me. She really knew how to work with young boys. That was the thing I really enjoyed about her. I remember she gave me a little book one time…*Little Philippe of Belgium*, a story about this little refugee in Europe and I found it inspiring. I never forgot that. It remains one of my favorite books.

I reflected a lot on her. I always wondered, "Why did she do that with me?" She must have realized that this kid needed a book like that…that this is what life is about to him. The book made an impression because this little boy was an independent little kid who got to where he was going on his own. *Little Philippe of Belgium.*

E. Maud Moles was the other huge influence from my school years. She was the math teacher in high school that got me going in calculus. She's also the first one who I remember telling me that I ought to be an engineer. You know, if your favorite teacher says you ought to be an engineer, you gravitate in that way. And I did well in those areas...National Honorary Society and things like that.

Wyandotte High and Sports

Wyandotte High was a fun experience for me. It was great. I had a few dates in high school, but girls and young women just were not on my radar yet. I did have a few suitors, but I matured pretty slowly.

My brothers, Don and Ken, and I about 1950

My neighbor, Roger Buford, was in my class. He was a big, heavyset guy on the football team, and he was pretty good. There was another guy by the name of Bill Strumillo who played at our high school on the team, and we used to shoot baskets at Park High School all the time. Bill was a wonderful guy. Allen Ditzen was the guy I went camping with. I had some really close friends in high school.

Ken, Don and I were all very athletic. I wasn't a big game guy…never played a lot of games other than pick-up games. Tennis and basketball, those were my two biggest sports.

Ken was quite good at football…he was all-city and maybe all-state. Don was a swimmer. I was on the basketball team at Wyandotte High School. I was better than average, but I didn't much like the coach.

All three of us played tennis. I didn't have lessons or any formal training. We played wherever we could – downtown at the park and the local high school. At Wyandotte High, Jack Hayden, a good friend of mine and later an outstanding dentist, and I were co-captains of the tennis team. We had no uniforms. We looked like a bunch of ragtag kids. Very seldom did any of the teams have uniforms. Jack and I traded off between one and two all year and we took the Wyandotte tennis team to the highest level that it has ever finished in the state, ending up second in the state finals to Topeka. I still regret losing to the Topeka number one, who was also number one in the state, because I had a lead and couldn't hold it. I ran into him not too long ago in a book group in Palo Alto. It was fun to reminisce.

Kansas Basketball Camp and Going to Stanford

When I was a kid, my dad and my brothers and I would go to Kansas football games. These were fun days. I enjoyed those trips up there. Of course, my dad had gone to Kansas. I did not know at the time about his extraordinary academic record at Kansas and Harvard. He never told anybody. It was probably a good thing I didn't know about it because I could have been intimidated by it. I was a pretty loosy-goosy kid.

My older brothers also went to Kansas. Don was drafted into the service right after high school before going to college and then went to Harvard Medical School. Ken went to Kansas first, then entered the service and gave them two years, serving, like me, as an officer in the Pacific fleet. When he got out of the service, he earned a civil engineering degree at Stanford and an MBA at Kansas. But the whole family was Kansans.

The thing was, ever since I had been a kid, as I've said, I was interested in getting out of Kansas. Don't get me wrong. I love Kansas. I had a wonderful childhood there, and I'm a very staunch Midwesterner. But have you ever been in Kansas in the middle of winter? It doesn't snow down, it snows sideways with the wind, and it's very cold. The summer can be 115 with 100% humidity without rain. I didn't want any part of that stuff. After that trip to California as a little boy, I thought California was the best place in the world to be. I thought that my whole life.

As a basketball player I was very aware of Stanford's team, because by the time I was applying to college, they had established a basketball tradition. In the late 1930s they had had Hank Luisetti, who is pretty much credited with inventing the one-handed jump shot. Up until that time, everyone shot a two-handed set shot, with both feet on the floor. In 1936, with Luisetti, Stanford beat Long Island University, the number one team in the country, at Madison Square Garden. That broke LIU's 43-game winning streak, and Luisetti's one-handed jump shot became a sensation. Then in 1938, they beat Duquesne 95-27, and Luisetti became the first guy ever to score 50 points in a game. That was almost twice what the entire Duquesne team had scored. Stanford went on to essentially win the unofficial national championship in 1938, which was the last year before they started the tournament. Then Stanford won that in 1942.

As a basketball player looking to college and wanting to return to California, that whole Stanford basketball tradition certainly got my attention. I was admitted to Kansas, but I had already talked to Stanford, and I had applied elsewhere as well: Georgia Tech, The Naval Academy, Cal Tech.

At the summer basketball camp I attended for state players and run by legendary Kansas Coach Phog Allen, Allen told me I wouldn't be making the team if I came to Kansas. But then he said, "I know you're interested in Stanford. I've written the basketball coach and I think you ought to go out there."

Dad was scared to death that he didn't have the money to fund a Stanford education. He flat out said he couldn't afford it, but I told him not to worry, that I'd figure it out. And I did. I found both a grant-in-aid academic scholarship, which they gave to people who really needed the money – which we really did – and a fellowship from an engineering firm in Kansas City called Burns and McDonald. They had a fellowship for Kansas and Missouri boys interested in engineering to go to Stanford. I would also have Navy funding once I joined the ROTC, and then I planned to work when I got there.

That summer before college I worked at my uncle's farm out in the country, about 13 miles south of Manhattan. This is part of the land my great-grandfather Gardner got after the Civil War. I still have a picture in my bedroom, which I also had at my house in Atherton, of a view south of Manhattan. It's beautiful, and I keep it as a reminder.

That fall of 1950 I left for Palo Alto, and my parents were absolutely happy I was going there. Dad was really, really proud. Like most kids headed off to college, I was just excited. But more than that, I was finally getting back to California, as I'd wanted since I was four, and I was going to Stanford!

RWM

Chapter Three:
Return to California...and Beyond
1950-58

Basketball at Stanford

The coach at Stanford in 1950-55 was Everett Dean, who had coached the team to the national championship in 1942. He also coached baseball. At that time freshmen couldn't play on the varsity, so there was a freshman team and a varsity team. Bob Burnett, the freshman coach, knew I was coming as part of the freshman team. He would eventually take over the varsity when Dean retired from coaching basketball to focus on baseball after my sophomore year, so we moved up together. I was initially sad that Dean retired but as fate would have it, two years later that all turned out to be a blessing.

My Stanford basketball team

During my freshman year I lived in Encina, a dorm near the quad which is now administrative offices. All freshmen had to live in dorms. One great story I remember from Encina involved a guy who removed the hugely long and flat fire hose, which was folded in a recess in the wall on the fourth or fifth floor and threaded it back and forth through the poles supporting the banister of the stairs going all the way to the ground floor. Then he found a way to turn the water on, and the hose immediately fattened from the top as the water powerfully coursed through it, which had the effect of blowing out the poles all the way down, five stories. It sounded like firecrackers and of course destroyed the railing. But it was cool...and totally irresponsible.

The next year I pledged ATO, where I lived for the rest of my time at Stanford. The last two years I was a resident assistant which meant I provided academic assistance to the younger guys in the house. Living at the ATO was less expensive, and it didn't cost Dad any money as I had my scholarships in place by then. The ATOs were mostly baseball players, and our team was quite good – number three in the country. The Zetes – Zeta Psi – were the football players, the Phi Psis were the basketball players, but at ATO we had eight of the starting nine on the baseball team. Jack Shepard was the catcher, and he went pro, as did Goodrich and Schwartz. Those guys were always up in front of the mirrors practicing their swings and I would go in there and practice my jump shot. It was fun, and we had a great time.

Stanford's academics in those days was mostly centered around the quad, the huge square made up of classroom buildings fronted on the interior by a columned corridor on all sides, with Memorial Church and its beautiful mural as the centerpiece. Engineering corner, where I had those classes, was at the far side of the quad from fraternity row, so it was a bit of a walk to class. I also took ROTC courses to get my scholarship from the Navy. These were military courses, officer training courses, and military history. The Navy was pretty serious, and it took me an extra quarter to complete all that. Between engineering and ROTC, I was essentially in a five-year bachelor's degree. Then I would owe the Navy three years of service.

I found a job hashing at the president's house, because one of my fraternity brothers, Chuck Getchall, was doing it, and needed a replacement. He was going back to Harvard to look at grad school or something, so I took his place and then they asked me to return the following year.

Hashing was basically serving the food for the president, Wallace Sterling, and his wife Anna, and particularly when they had guests, which

ATO House on the Stanford campus

were often Nobel Prize winners, outstanding professors, business leaders and so on. I hashed when Robert Frost, John Kennedy, Dwight Eisenhower, Herbert Hoover, and many notables were there. It was a pretty sweet deal because Sterling had a policy of asking his guests to recognize that Stanford was an academic institution, teaching was a 24-hour business, the hashers were students working their way through school and that this was part of their education. Then he would always invite whoever the guest was to have a conversation with the hashers after dinner. We would serve the last round of coffee and the dessert, change into a clean apron, and get a half hour or so with the guest...whoever it was. Think about that! College kids meeting with presidents and other people like that in extended casual conversations.

Sterling gave us just one instruction: "Don't embarrass me," which roughly translated into "Don't screw up." Keep in mind what we had to do in that day and age. A guy like Robert Frost comes down, but I'm an engineer and I don't know who Robert Frost is. We don't have these magic little things like Google and the internet you can use to get a history of something in five minutes. We had to go to the daggone library and find out the latest news stories or manuscripts and check them out and do research. It was a pain, but we did it. We learned how to use the library very efficiently, as much through meeting with Sterling's guests as through our studies, by breaking the subject matter up into disciplines to find and evaluate the subject at hand.

Kennedy was really fun. He was just a senator, I think, at the time. He related to us because he was very young. The war had just been over a short time. In fact, it really wasn't over with at all because Korea was going on. Eisenhower was President at that time, and I talked to him as well.

Dr. Sterling was a very influential man. He was a big guy maybe 6'4", with huge hands. Absolutely huge. He was a Canadian and his field was art history. No kidding. He'd gotten a doctorate in art history at Stanford and then worked for a while at the Hoover Institution. He went to Cal Tech and then left there to head up the Huntington Library and Art Gallery, which was where he was when the Stanford trustees tapped him to be president.

I think some people took some convincing that he was the right guy for the job, but boy was he ever! They made a beautiful selection in that guy. He was there 20 years, from 1949 to 1968, and he really set Stanford on the path to success. Stanford was apparently having some financial struggles when he arrived, but when he left in 1968 it was financially very solid, partially as a result of three things Sterling initiated: first, he built the Stanford Shopping Center on leased University land, which generated significant cash flow to the University; second, he launched the Stanford Research Park, which attracted government grants and was fundamental to the development of Silicon Valley; and third, he started PACE, the largest fundraising program ever undertaken by any university up to that time, and with which I later was involved.

Stanford's international reputation also went through the roof under Sterling, who moved the medical school from San Francisco to the campus, created the overseas campus program and built the bookstore, post office, student union, dormitories, a faculty club, and many academic buildings. The student body grew by 40% during his tenure, but the faculty grew by almost 300%, which of course dramatically lowered the faculty-student ratio.

Perhaps Sterling's most significant contribution to Stanford was hiring Fred Terman as provost. Terman had two students getting their PhDs at MIT. Later he called Bill Hewlett and David Packard back to Stanford and everyone knows what happened next. Sterling and Terman are the real founders of Silicon Valley.

Wallace Sterling was there my whole time at Stanford. I got to know him very well and he had a huge impact on me. He talked to us all the time. He was marvelous, and Mrs. Sterling was dynamic too, and a very gracious lady. Helga and I remained good friends with them for years.

Summers

During the summer after my freshman year, I worked at the Armour Meat Packing Company back in Kansas City, which was the year of the great flood. Due to extremely heavy rains in May and June, the Kansas and the Missouri Rivers were at peak by July and finally overtopped the dikes...just went right over the top. The stockyards and West Bottoms were underwater. The downtown airport was flooded which caused TWA to move to a new airport way north of town in Platte County, which eventually became Kansas City International Airport. Overall, about a million acres were flooded in both Kansas and Missouri, and in both states a significant amount of the houses were just ruined.

We knew the owner of the lumber yard in the Argentine area of town. As the waters were rising, he asked the Corps of Engineers if the dikes would hold, and they said yes. When he got that answer, he left his lumber in the Bottomland. BIG MISTAKE. The next day he saw his lumber go down to New Orleans....for free.

In the end, the damage approached a billion dollars – nearly nine billion dollars today. Seventeen people died and half a million lost their homes. We of course lost our jobs, but then some of us got hired back on by the government to do clean up. Not a fun job...the filth was just horrific. During the flood, as a member of the maintenance staff, I saw thousands of rats swarm out of the sewers and into the streets. It was a sight I'll never forget. The cleaning of the mess afterwards involved cleaning up animal carcasses and muck all over the place.

During another summer, John Skillman, a fraternity brother, and I worked for Santa Fe Railroad back in Kansas. I was a switchman and a gandy dancer, which is a guy that goes along with men doing rail repair on the black ties that the rail sits on. You basically take a tool like a great big ice pick, dig it in beside that tie, and shove it out so it falls down by the side. But those things are heavy…really heavy. You've got to make damn sure that you are not in the way of that tie falling. If you're dealing with a stack of these things, you can break your leg, so you "gandy dance" out of the way. Hence the name, "gandy dancers." John went to Harvard Medical School and became an orthopedic surgeon back in Boston. He is now retired and writes poetry. I've read it all and it's very, very good.

Meeting Helga

I didn't date much at Stanford because I was a very serious student. Between engineering, ROTC, basketball and hashing I didn't have a lot of free time. Then in my junior year, I saw this really attractive girl, the centerfold in the *Chaparral*, which was a student magazine. I thought, "I must

Helga Biermer, my future wife, as she appeared in the Stanford Chaparral Magazine, where I first saw her.

meet this woman. She's so beautiful!" I noticed she'd gone to high school in Burlingame, where my fraternity brother, Don Curry had gone, so I asked if he could introduce me. He said, "Yeah, sure. I have history class with her. Meet me at history corner tomorrow at 11:55 when we get out and I'll introduce you."

The Peninsula Creamery, still an institution in downtown Palo Alto, where Helga and I had our first date

So, on the 11th of March 1953 at 11:55, I met this wonderful woman. And...BOOM! I was literally crazy in love from that moment. I couldn't believe how lucky I was. I knew that was the girl I wanted. I didn't know quite how to handle that, so I asked her if she would join me for coffee that night and she said, "Yes". We drove down to the Peninsula Creamery in Palo Alto

I had a hot chocolate, but I was so heady to be there that I don't have the slightest idea what we talked about. We were both juniors, and she was studying econ and foreign relations. She was an outstanding student, had straight A's and was magna cum laude. She was brilliant. Just brilliant.

Helga had gone to Pomona for two years because Stanford required people living within 25 miles to live at home, because at that time there was still a university housing shortage, and she didn't want to do that. After two years she transferred up and lived in Stillman House, one of several women's houses on Mayfield right near Tresidder Union near the back of the campus. It turned out that a bunch of ATOs like Don Curry dated girls at Stillman, and some of those couples married and remained close friends for years. I was just very lucky to have Don get me a date with Helga, who I lost in 2018 after 67 years, 62 of which we were married.

At the end of the first date at the Peninsula Creamery, she was absolutely magnificent in respect. Interestingly, it turned out that I'd forgotten my wallet and didn't have any money. She started kidding around with me. "Are you sure you didn't intentionally not bring your wallet?" Helga saved me, as she would do numerous times. Harbinger of things to come. She was absolutely magnificent.

The Stillman House where Helga lived

The Crossroads

About the same time that I met Helga, I made the varsity and played one year in Encina Gym, which preceded the current gym, Maples Pavilion. That was fun. I loved Stanford basketball, but it was tough on me principally because engineering labs took up every afternoon. I had to cut this and cut that practice, and Coach Burnett wasn't particularly happy about that. He didn't see my pain. I felt I was just fodder in his eyes. I was also getting aced out on court by Ron Tomsich, an All-American who would win a gold medal in the Olympics with Hank Iba. George Selleck was also competing for my spot.

Just as I was struggling with balancing basketball and my academics, not playing as much as I wanted and thinking about a future with Helga, and how to support

Helga and I while we were dating

this fabulous girl I was dating, my engineering professor, Clark Oglesby who eventually became my mentor and great friend, confronted me. He said, "Bob, you've got to make some basic decisions. Are you going to play basketball or are you going to be an engineer? You can't do both."

I already had a decision-making process driven into me by my dad: "look at the facts and make an analysis of what is going on and where you want to go." Oglesby was basically asking me where I wanted to go, and the answer was clear to me. "I want to be an engineer," I told him.

The rest of the process was easy. The facts were that basketball did not have the future that engineering did. Not much to analyze there, so it was an easy decision. Helga helped make the decision too, and then she helped me get even more serious about my studies. She would say, "We're going to go to the library. No fooling around! You are studying." And she meant it!

Helga and I dated all spring semester, and then a guy she had been seeing in Pomona told her that he was planning to come up and see her. She was, thankfully, no longer interested in him, and assured me that she loved me, but she felt she had to talk to the gentleman face to face. I understood that and even loaned her my car for the weekend. I wanted her to be in safe hands. There was no question of loyalty. I thought it was typical of Helga to want to do it the right and most gentle way.

That summer I didn't go back to Kansas. No way! I lived right at the ATO house. I kept hashing at

My ATO brothers at Stanford

Sterling's House that summer, and I was working on my civil engineering license. For work, I was hired to do drafting design and preliminary engineering work with James Breen Co., an engineering firm in the Bay area. That summer we worked on the stretch of bypass on 101 going into South San Francisco where the freeway cuts across the landfill. We did all the engineering developing the curve line of the road. There were a lot of subdivisions going into Millbrae at the time and I also did some surveying work on them.

Half of one summer, about six weeks, as a part of my ROTC training, I went on a midshipman's cruise, because the Navy wanted us to have experience on board a ship by the time we graduated and entered the service. We went through the Caribbean and to Trinidad and a bunch of other ports. Sam Morley, an All-American wide receiver for Stanford and Eric Mack were good friends who were also on the ship, so we had a great time together on our midshipman's cruise.

Stanford was terrific. I liked all the subjects, and I obviously did better in some than others. There were a bunch of really bright people at Stanford...the people you meet there are just extraordinary. I didn't ever dream how wise that decision was to go there. It was that environment which made me who I am, and I wouldn't have met Helga if I hadn't gone to Stanford. But in addition, I had Oglesby and Sterling. Those three people saved my life...going there was by far and away the wisest decision I ever made.

Neither Helga nor I, by the way, ever dated anyone else after our first date at the Peninsula Creamery. I stayed two more years. I took five years to graduate, because I was an engineer and in ROTC. In subsequent years we used to go back to the Creamery on March 11th if we were in town. I'd have a milkshake, though, instead of a hot chocolate.

One of the wonderful things about coming to the University Retirement Center (URC) here in 2018 is that I can order my milkshakes at the outdoor eating area, Le Bistro...a great tradition in my closing years.

The Navy

After graduation in 1955 I owed the Navy three years and Helga was training to be a nurse up in San Francisco. We lived together up there, some of the first people that did that

Helga served as a nurse while I was in the service

before they got married. My parents knew that and were okay with it because they'd met Helga and loved her.

I was stationed on the *USS Los Angeles CE135*, which is the classification of the ship: a Baltimore class heavy cruiser. It carried 1,142 officers and enlisted personnel. I was an ensign, which is a commissioned officer ranking just above chief warrant officer and below lieutenant. Later I was promoted to lieutenant JG., and then during my years in the reserves, while I was in Arizona, I was promoted to full lieutenant. I filled out the requirements for lieutenant commander but that took too much time, so I dropped out of the reserves, in 1964, almost ten years of military service with three years active duty.

On the *Los Angeles* I served as the ship's education, intelligence and information officer. The education officer gets all the manuals for the people in the right spot at the right time. You're basically involved in continuing education. It's a make-work job.

The intelligence part was better, because it required studies in cryptography, which I studied on base before joining my ship. Not too many people would be doing cryptographic work at that time, and I greatly enjoyed my training in this area. I felt the Navy had preferences for guys from Rensselaer Polytechnic, MIT, Cal Tech and Stanford for classified and cryptographic work. It was a wonderful job and very good for me because it was so very different from normal duties.

Ensign Robert C. Medearis, USN

Our captain was Captain Lucas. You get to know the captain pretty well if you are in navigation or information because you are always interfacing with him. Lucas liked to play tennis, so he and I played a lot of tennis together at officers' clubs when we were in port. You're treated like royalty at these places. The officers have it pretty easy, but it's been that way since Napoleon's time.

I was on two long cruises. When I joined the *Los Angeles*, the ship was in the open Pacific, off of Korea. I joined it at sea which was a fun deal because I flew from Travis Air Force Base near San Francisco to Hawaii, and then went by Naval airplane from Hawaii to Guam, which was in the midst of a typhoon that eventually devastated China.

The USS Los Angeles, a Baltimore Class heavy cruiser on which I served as an ensign in the Asian theater during the mid-1950s

I had to wait for five days at the base on Guam for it to blow itself out, but in the meantime the eye passed right over us, and suddenly the weather was beautiful. I was thinking, "What's happening? Where did the storm go?"

Another sailor told me that we had about four hours of beautiful weather and then the second half of the typhoon would hit, and it would be worse. So he and I went out and played handball. I was just out of basketball and I thought I was going to wax this guy, but he ran me all over. We were showering and cleaning up and getting ready for the other side of the storm when he said, "Don't feel too badly, ensign. I'm the Navy handball champion." He really knew where to place that ball. It was a great lesson in humility.

When the storm passed, I flew by plane from Guam to an aircraft carrier, the *Lexington*. They put me up one or two days until we got close enough to the *Los Angeles* for those of us who were joining it to chopper over. We were doing fleet operations and ships were spread out all over the ocean.

The helicopter that left the *Lexington* right before mine hit a downdraft and dunked in the ocean. They lost both men aboard. I saw it happen. It scared me to death. I said, "You aren't going to get me in one of those things."

The helicopter pilot just said, "Yes, sir. Now get in, ensign. We're taking off."

Fortunately, we didn't hit any downdrafts and reached the *Los Angeles* safely. It was cruising about 10 knots and riding the waves, and my suitcases and I were lowered down onto the foc'sle, or the forward upper deck. How is that for joining your ship at sea? You'd think that I was important.

The fighting had been pretty well concluded in Korea two years before, in 1953, but we were technically involved in combat when I got there because we were still shelling. We would go in from 14 or 15 miles off the coast and shell, because the closer you are the better you could pinpoint the target, and then head back out. The Navy had people on active duty therefore the next ten years.

In 1956, we began patrolling the Taiwan Strait in what were called "peace-keeping" operations, and protecting friendly Taiwanese, or Republic of China army units from aggression by our mutual enemy, Communist China. That fall we had an interesting trip taking the *USS Los Angeles* up the Saigon River into the heart of Saigon. Everything was friendly at that time, but we did that because Eisenhower wanted to show the flag. It was just a show of strength and solidarity with South Vietnam which was also at risk (as was clearly demonstrated about ten years later) from encroachment by Communist China and Russia through North Vietnam.

We worried a lot about Russia and were monitoring a lot of data on what Russia was doing, but the intelligence we were getting about all that was really queer. Really strange. We would get a report that said one thing and then we would get a report that said exactly the opposite. In hindsight, I think we were being fed misinformation.

When we crossed from ocean to river, the ship dropped precipitously, about two feet, because saltwater is denser, and hence more buoyant than fresh water. In other words, the ship sank deeper in the less buoyant water once we got out of the sea and into the river. I don't think the powers that be had calculated for this, because we were scraping bottom a lot as we sailed upriver. We got through the river, periodically scraping the bottom.

When we got to Saigon and a tug swung us around so we could face downstream for a quicker exit. After three days in port showing the flag, the brass put on a big dinner. We were all lined up and the officers were there in our formal dresses and so on. It was a bunch of show and

I resented it. I kept saying, "What a waste this all is!" It was just a dog and pony show. Eisenhower wanted to show solidarity with the existing government, which was really a message to North Vietnam and Russia…particularly Russia, but I got really upset at the waste of it all.

The irony of that is that we were already aligned with South Vietnam because they had been fighting China for the last 600 years. Then we completely screwed that relationship up. To be honest, I'm pretty bitter about the way we handled those things at that time. This was in essence a forerunner to the Vietnam war, and at the time, after being there, it seemed patently obvious to me that we should not in any way get involved in Vietnam. I've talked to my good friend Alain Enthoven, who was undersecretary of defense to Robert McNamara, about this a year later, and after our discussions I knew I was not alone in my feelings.

The next thing that happened was that the Suez Crisis broke out when Egyptian President Gamal Nasser nationalized the British-owned Suez Canal, and in order to regain western control of the canal Israel, France and the UK invaded, with support from the U.S. We had to high tail it down the Saigon River, go through the straits around the south side of Vietnam and go through the Malacca Strait between Malaysia and Singapore to get over to the Indian Ocean. From there it was a straight shot to the Suez. The Navy wanted us to be a nuclear ship, so we carried nuclear weaponry all the way to Suez.

On that trip we carried Admiral Wright and his Chief of Staff P.T. Buckley. Buckley was a good officer for whom I had a great deal of respect; he had taken

McArthur out of the Philippines at the beginning of World War II.

That whole trip from Vietnam to the Suez was a very interesting exercise. They told us we would have air cover all the way, and we did, but it wasn't friendly aircraft! It was Bisons – Russian long-range bombers. It was funny, actually. I don't think we were in any danger, but then you never know.

War gets started over the stupidest mistakes. If two sides start beating on each other, accidents happen. I can't reveal all that I

The Myasishchev M-4, also known as the Bison, Russia's long-range bomber, flew regular missions over our ship.

picked up on those missions because I was sworn to absolute total secrecy, and there is no expiration on that. Suffice to say I got a lot of data, and it was downright scary, partially because it comes down to people's idiosyncrasies and their often-faulty decision-making process.

The Navy was a good job which I enjoyed thoroughly. After two cruises we went to Yokohama and then in 1957 we came home to San Francisco because we had a lot of reconditioning to do on the ship, which was done at Long Beach and Vallejo, California.

Helga and I Marry

Helga was getting her master's in nursing from UC San Francisco and living in an apartment building in San Francisco. That was our home, but I was on the ship.

Right when we got to Long Beach for our first recondition, I took a leave and came home to get married. I moved back in with Helga.

On February 7th, two days before the wedding, my brother Ken and three or four guys took me out for dinner. I don't remember who else was there besides my brother. Don couldn't be there because he was tied up with internships. We went to L'Omelette, which everybody called "L'Ommies" a little one-story restaurant on El Camino in south Palo Alto that was famous for its abalone. It's gone now.

That's the only time I've really been drunk in my life; I just had too many martinis. It was a very unpleasant experience. I was a very sick boy. That was the end of my drinking. Now I have a glass of wine or a glass of sherry and an occasional beer with lots of ice in it, but those were the last hard liquor drinks I've ever had. I drink my beer on the rocks now.

Two days later, on Feb 9, less than four years after we had first met at History Corner at Stanford, Helga and I were married. The service was held at her

Helga and I on our wedding day

family's Lutheran Church in Burlingame, and both our families were there. Ken was my best man.

We honeymooned at The Thunderbird in Palm Springs. We just had fun being together. It was a great time. We ate and slept and drank and frolicked. We were there a week-and-a-half before I rejoined the ship. I was totally in love with Helga. A more magnificent person I have never known. I miss her greatly after her sudden death two years ago.

I came back to California one more time for about three or four months while I was in the service when the ship underwent a second reconditioning in Vallejo. That was a lot of fun. A guy named Charlie Sandberg, a Zete from Stanford, was a jock who was on the *Los Angeles* with me. Charlie was our athletic officer, and there were about seven or eight officers that were all former college athletes. We all thought we were a lot better than we were in all the sports, so we signed up for everything Charlie cooked up. Wherever there was an Army or a Marine Corp base, he set up a tournament. He arranged for

Scuba diving while our ship was stationed in California

volleyball at Alameda, Treasure Island, the Presidio, baseball...anything he could set up. We were never aboard the ship. I was an officer still working on various projects, but I still had time to get off. It was just a riot and it kept us in good shape.

I also took the opportunity to take classes in computer science and anything else of interest the Navy offered at a couple of schools at bases around the Bay. It was not hard duty at all. I played all athletics all the time, went to school and took advantage of all the things you can take advantage of in the Bay Area. Just as I'd dreamed of 20 years before!

A Bump in the Road

Before going into the service, I had applied and was admitted to Harvard Business School. I planned to attend when I got out of the service because at the time they had a policy of "once admitted, always admitted." During my second year in the Navy, therefore, I sent a letter back to Harvard which said I was getting out the following year, in the late summer of 1957 and would be starting that fall. I got a message back that said, in short, "Oh no, you're not."

I was stunned. I immediately responded that I had been told that the policy was, "once admitted, always admitted." But they responded that that was now an outdated policy, and it didn't apply to me.

We then commenced a real go-around, mainly over the phone lines, which was expensive, because I was in Guam at that point. Somewhat panicking, I said, "I've been in the service for three years knowing that I was going to go to Harvard Business School, and now you're telling me I'm not admitted?" I was probably shouting so loudly they could have heard me from Guam without the phone. "What does it take for me to be admitted?" I asked, continuing to remind them all along that I had already been admitted once.

The administrator, whoever he was, told me I had to take the exam again. More upset than ever, I shouted, "I don't have the money to come back there and take the exam again! I'm in the Navy in Guam, 16,000 miles from nowhere!"

I shouldn't have told poor Helga about this, because she worried about it. She was naturally worried that we didn't know where we were going to go or what we were going to do. I told her, "I'll be at Harvard next year. Count on it. Don't worry about it. We will figure it out."

Privately of course I really didn't have a plan at all, so I called my dad, explained the circumstances, and asked him what he'd do. He told me to call Deane Mallott, who was the president of Cornell and the former president of University of Kansas. Mallott and my father were trustees at Kansas together and our families knew each other pretty well. Dad said that Mallott was a wonderful guy, an honest guy, and he'd help.

I remember saying, "Are you sure, Dad?"

He said, "Yes, trust me on this one."

So I called Mallott, explained the situation, and told him I was beside myself on what to do. He said, "Let me call Dean Baker at Harvard Business School and I'll get back to you."

The next day I got a phone call from Mallott who asked if I'd agree to take the exam when I got back?

"Yes," I said

"Will you take a leave early to do it? "

"Yes sir, I will."

He said, "That's a good answer. Call Dean Baker and you tell him exactly that."

I called Dean Baker, whom I didn't know at all, and we talked. He also asked if I would come back early and take the exam. I told him that I would but that I was planning on paying my own way at Harvard and that it would be a huge financial penalty on me to fly back and do that.

He then backed off a little and asked if I would take the exam when I got there at the regular time? I said yes again, and he said, "I'll let you know tomorrow my decision," and hung up.

The next day I got a decision. Baker said I could come back at my leisure. I was in. Forget about the exam. That was pretty darn nice of him, because I thought they weren't going to let me in. I was wondering what I was going to do for the next two years. Helga was very relieved.

The stage was set for the next steps in my life: family life, start-ups, entrepreneurship, and teaching.

RWM

Chapter Four
Harvard Business School, 1958-60

When we finally got to Boston, Helga, who had gotten her master's in nursing in California, got a job at Mass General Hospital. Her primary field of interest was actually in treating bulimia and anorexia, and she eventually did a lot of work in that area, but in Boston she was in general nursing.

We lived on Pearl Street in Cambridge, which at the time was a somewhat run-down section of Cambridge on the north side of the Charles. We were about four blocks away from the Business School, and I'd walk down and cross the bridge to class. The football stadium was about two more blocks up on the right. It was an easy walk, but often very cold.

The first year at B-school you can only take required courses, which wasn't that interesting. In the summer between my first and second year I got a job at Buildings and Grounds at MIT, courtesy of Dick Balch, who had been Dean of Men at Stanford before becoming the athletic director at MIT. That was a real switch for him, as MIT was not known like Stanford for its athletic teams.

I loved Dick Balch, and he really did me a huge favor because that was the best summer job I think I've ever had. I formed contracts for cutting grasses, for building buildings, for changing things around. Everything that came under outside construction and maintenance activities was my responsibility. It was a huge job, but I had a great time, and Helga and I even managed to take a two-week vacation.

Late in the summer the guy that ran the whole Building and Grounds Department had a heart attack and never came back. They wanted me to stay on, but I told them I couldn't because I had to go back to school. They finally talked me into staying an extra month while they conducted a search for the new head of the department, so I made them promise not to tell Harvard. The first month of fall semester in my second and final year at HBS, therefore, I was doing these two things. Harvard generally hated it if you did that, and eventually they found out. Dr. Baker, the associate dean, really let me have it!

I thank the good Lord that Dick Balsch got me that job; I was very indebted to him because I was very lucky to have it. I made good money, and it was a really great life experience about what goes on in the real world. In short, the job allowed me to expand in a different direction: thinking about how you motivate field workers in the inculcation of new ideas, processes and procedures. That stuck with me the rest of my life. I still go through machinations of those types of issues in my head today.

The Second Year

The second year was the highlight because we had some flexibility. I took my first really inspiring course at HBS that year, and it was called "Production". It was about starting businesses and was taught by a professor named George Doriot. This was the first venture capital experience I had ever had, and it was life changing. I picked it knowingly because I'd heard great things about this guy, which stemmed from both his teaching and his background. At age 21, Doriot had sailed by steamship to the U.S. from his home in France and went on to become a brigadier general in the Second World War. Later he founded Europe's first business school. Most importantly, in 1946 he essentially invented the U.S. venture capital industry by setting up American Research & Development (ARD), which backed one of the first blockbuster technology start-ups, Digital Equipment Corporation. By the time I took his class in Production, he was of the most influential professors at Harvard Business School. If you asked anyone who had his class who was the most influential teacher there, they would have said it was Doriot. Certainly he was the first venture capitalist to teach there.

I can't say that Doriot's Production course is where I began thinking about starting companies, because there had long been an entrepreneurial seed planted in my psyche. That's why the course appealed to me, and I was at Harvard to learn something new, not develop my engineering. I'd had that background, and I was already a good engineer, so when he said, on the first day of class, "I'm going to tell you how a business really runs," I was happy. He had lived the life that he was talking about, and this really resonated with me. From that first day the whole course stimulated my entrepreneurial interests.

Not surprisingly, Doriot was a different type of teacher, very entrepreneurial in the classroom, and I was impressed with his unusual (for HBS) modus operandi of lecturing instead of presenting case studies. He just didn't use cases. Teachers who use case studies discuss the cases instead of lecturing. One time we met with him and asked him what would happen if everybody lectured and he said, "Then I'd teach by the case." He was determined to be different.

Doriot, though, was a very good lecturer and certainly fun to listen to. I learned a lot from his approach, which required taking copious notes. Ultimately, he was the teacher, far more than any other, who changed the way I looked at things, and his course altered my whole approach to business. Oglesby at Stanford was a traditionalist, but Doriot was a maverick, and that made a huge difference for me. He taught me that you don't stick with the traditional stuff if you don't feel like it. Instead, you rely on your instincts. These ideas expanded on the ones I already had about rules, which boiled down to something along the lines of, "You are good at what you do. Trust it, do it, and to heck with anything else." A lot of us followed Doriot's precepts, and in so doing I learned some incredible life lessons, which I used the rest of my life. For instance, I came to the realization that if I was going to be successful, I would have to like what I was doing; consequently, when I later found myself in environments that I didn't like, I got out, sometimes at great expense.

I had other great teachers, of course. I went over to MIT to take a course from Enrique Catalano. Harvard hated that when they found out. He was an expert on eggshell design, and his course was on a pre-stressed concrete design, which was something that Frank Lloyd Wright later picked up on. I also had Malcolm McNair at Harvard for marketing. He was a brilliant marketing guy, a wonderful guy to listen to, but he didn't have the genuine "I've been there" approach that Doriot had.

The Group Report

In Doriot's class we formed groups. Our group had two guys from small colleges in the east, a guy by the name of Schultz who graduated from West Point, and Scott York, who was an architectural student who was a dear friend. Finally, there was Gordon Smith who also became a very dear, lifelong friend, and David Miller, who became Gordon's business partner in Washington D.C. at Miller and Smith, a homebuilder group. As he did with me, Doriot really resonated with Miller and Smith.

Doriot gave us all a single assignment: a group report to develop a business plan and a strategy for the inculcation for that business in society. We were to get together collectively as a group and determine a topic that we wanted to do. This was basically our thesis, and all our individual grades would depend on how the group as a whole did on the report. The other guys thought they wanted to do something in electronics, but they were also a bit uncertain, and kept hemming and hawing. I wasn't very interested in that because I'd already sketched out a report for industrializing homebuilding. Still, I said, "Guys, I'll go along with you and help, but I've already written the genesis for the whole thing on this other subject."

I had actually been thinking about homebuilding long before Doriot's class, as early as when I was taking Clark Oglesby's courses as an undergraduate at Stanford. Later, when I was in the service, I pretty much decided that that was what I wanted to do because at night I had

had lots of free time on the ship, sailing through the South China Sea, to think about it. We were all by ourselves on this vast ocean, and I would take walks up to the fo'c'sle and the bow, and then I'd sit there and think about who I was and what I was doing and why I was doing it. I was an engineer, and I liked to build things, and at one point I thought that maybe I'd be a bridge builder. I loved the design and the choreography of building a bridge, but I kept thinking more deeply about it…about what good was in what I was doing.

As I was pondering these questions, it's important to realize the huge impact Stanford President Wallace Sterling and his dean, Fred Terman, had already made on my thinking. Back when I was hashing at his house as a student, Sterling had recognized that he had these incredible guests, and had decided that the students like me working there should have 35 minutes with them after every dinner. I was impressed with how creative that was. It was really neat, because Sterling decided to make use of this opportunity. He was asking himself questions about the role of a university and found an additional and powerful chance for students to learn. He was right on top of it! Sterling was creative and wise, and he guided a lot of others who bought into his whole vision.

Terman was very similar. An electrical engineer professor he helped transform Stanford into a world-class university. Then he and a lot of venture capitalists, all creative, brilliant people, helped create what became Silicon Valley.

All these people created something where nothing had existed. That is where Stanford was so good. My professor and mentor Clark Olglesby had also been a genius in that, and to this day I lay in bed and fall asleep thinking about how I can do something better.

I realized that the key in all these cases was in finding opportunities and then thinking creatively about how to take advantage of them. For me personally it suggested something at the nexus of engineering and entrepreneurship. Boiling all these questions and thoughts down to a career path was what I was thinking about on board the ship all those nights: where was the good in what I could do, in engineering, and where I could entrepreneurial. Where could I be creative and make a difference?

The answer was homebuilding, and it came out of simply looking around and realizing that at that time, in 1958, there were all these veterans coming home from Korea on top of waves of veterans that had returned after World War II. I knew these returning servicemen had created—and were still creating—a pent-up demand for housing. There was a great need for quality, affordable living units across the entire country. That long-standing and still unabated need had recently begun to result in the suburbanization of America. Everything was tied into it: jobs, a need for creativity within the building process, the availability of land. But it all boiled down to one thing: how do you efficiently, economically and effectively make well-constructed housing on a mass basis?

Helga had helped immensely for the five years we had been together as I had thought through all this. I'd married not only the most wonderful woman in the world, but a brilliant person and a great sounding board. She never, ever criticized anything I did, even though she had a lot of room to had she wished. Instead, she went with me to the ends of the earth. But she certainly played devil's advocate on many things, and certainly on my ideas about homebuilding. In so doing, she had contributed greatly to my thought process.

By the spring of my second year at Harvard, therefore, my thoughts about the future of homebuilding had been seven years in the making: two at Stanford, three in the service and the last two years at Harvard. And they had only accelerated in Doriot's class about new businesses. The report was the opportunity to develop a serious business plan out of these ideas.

Unfortunately, the rest of my group thought they wanted to do a report on electronics, a subject about which I was uninterested. Despite my passion for homebuilding, I was a team player, and was learning to let go of my own ideas in support of the group. I said to the other guys, "Here's what I'd like to do, but I'll defer to the group if you come up with something better." I didn't want to just shove my own idea through, so I just walked away from it.

In the end, with the deadline approaching, they came back and said, "We don't have anything. Can we use your report?"

I just said "Here it is. Let's go."

The report for Doriot's class on homebuilding turned out to be pretty damn good paper. It was well received and is in the Library of Congress. Incredibly, it also served as the catalyst for what each one of us in the group would become. Everybody in that group— everyone! —went into housing. I thought that was amazing, and I took a lot of pride in the fact that it was my idea that helped shape all of our future careers. Ultimately, I got my first job at Lusk in Arizona out of that class, a job I don't think I would have landed without it. It changed David Miller's and Gordon Smith's whole direction, because they later founded Miller and Smith which was a homebuilding company in Washington D.C. and made a fortune. Gordon Smith is a very wealthy man today. Miller and Smith still exists, but Gordon is retired, and his family now owns it all and runs it. Gordon and I became lifetime friends and kept doing partnerships together.

I ended up with an A+ in Doriot's class, I think because I was one of the guys most like him. I think that there was a kinship between the two of us as mavericks that he saw, but which I didn't recognize until later.

The moral of the group report story for me was that by simply following my own drummer, I realized I was being a pretty good leader as well. Maybe that is what I'm good for: guiding people into productive work. I thought a lot about that. But the real key to this leadership—and I have given a lot of thought to this, too—was learning to let go.

RWM

Chapter Five
The Lusk Years, 1960-67

Job Search

When it came time to interview for jobs, I was interested in only two who were interviewing students at HBS: Stanley Works and Lusk Corporation. Stanley Works made tools— hammers, saws, etc.— and a guy by the name of Garth Edwards was the vice president. I interviewed with him and boy, I liked that company. I liked what he was doing. But you go through all sorts of mental machinations about what it is you want to do, and I finally told him that tools was not close to what I wanted to do. I wanted to be closer to building and construction. Also, Stanley was a Massachusetts-based company, and I didn't want to be in Massachusetts.

Lusk was down in Tucson, Arizona, and that sounded really good to me. So was the fact that they were was doing creative things in the building business. They built massive subdivisions, bridges, retention dams and all kinds of cool stuff. It was a company I thought I could really resonate with, and they were hiring Harvard

Business School guys. Most importantly, they were open to hiring creative, entrepreneurial people.

The president and founder Bob Lusk came out to Cambridge and interviewed about nine or ten of us at HBS. He was a creative guy and I really liked him too. We talked a lot about the whole process, and I finally said, "Well, I've made my decision. If you want me, I'm coming." I think he liked the fact that I was a licensed professional engineer, which was a great two-fer for him.

He hired me and also a guy by the name of Bill Baker, who was in a different section than mine. I really liked Bill and we became very friendly over the years.

Lusk

Lusk was a pretty good-sized company, and it turned that there were a bunch of guys from Harvard Business School there, though not all of us entered at the same time. Boyd Prior, vice president of sales and marketing, was a very brilliant marketing guy; Russ Wild, the chief financial officer who had fought in the Battle of the Bulge, was not Harvard, but his associate, Jerry Thomas, was. Ted Steele, senior VP, had gone there. Finally, there was Bill Baker, who ended up running the Phoenix market when I ran Tucson. We were all very close while working at Lusk. Steele, Wild and Pryer are all gone now, but the last time I heard, Bill Baker, who did very well as a builder after Lusk, was living in Chappaqua, New York.

Helga and I had had Ken, our first child, while we were at Harvard, so after graduation I left the two of them with her parents, Herman and Hilde in Hillsborough, California, just south of San Francisco, and rented a very small two-bedroom, one-bath house in Tucson. Two years later we built a home on Mesa Grande in a subdivision named Indian Ridge by the Mesa Verde River in north Tucson. Once I had the house, Helga and Ken came down and joined me.

Watching our first-born, Ken, playing on the stoop of our house in Tucson

Helga's roommate from Pomona was the wife of a big rancher, Fred Boice, who lived in the area. They made introductions for us to the community and that just integrated us so fast it was unbelievable. It is people like that and our next-door neighbors, the Hinkles, both of whom became lifelong friends, that really open the door for you.

We had Ilsi while we lived in the Mesa Grande house. This was about the best place for a young couple to start and we really had a great time. Tucson is a beautiful city and a lot cooler than Phoenix. The University of Arizona was there so there was a lot of growth taking place. I think the university was about 15,000 students then. Today it must be about 45,000. I vowed then that I would always live in a town with a good university, and over the next 50 years we ended up living in Tucson, Palo Alto and Davis – all really great college towns.

The Lusk Corporation

Lusk had fully integrated the building business, and we didn't work for anybody else. We worked only for ourselves and did everything as a homebuilder. We had our own mortgage company, our own finance company, and our own building company. We handled all the services in providing low-income housing and subdivisions for a vast number of people.

These were all entrepreneurial subdivisions all throughout Arizona, New Mexico and elsewhere. For instance, we were in Nogales and Kokomo, Indiana, which was a very successful project that Ted Steele did a good job running. Basically, we would go out and buy land, develop it and build thousands and thousands of houses in a way we thought would best serve the needs of the marketplace at the time. We really had a pretty good building business.

We built all sorts of houses and had a custom home division that I ran called Lusk Custom Homes. Everything we built we also sold ourselves to individual homebuyers. That was where I started, because when I got there, Bob Lusk said, "I want you to go into sales." This was the genius of Lusk. He was pretty creative because he wanted me to know the building industry from all sides. He said, "You know the construction side. You know the engineering side. You know the land development side. What you don't know is the sales and the product side." I was scared to death about this and at first it didn't make sense to me, but he was right; I needed to learn it because I hadn't done it before. It was new, and I loved that. I loved anything new.

We would advertise in the morning and evening newspapers and put up signs on the weekend that we were opening a subdivision in a desert. That was a constant marketing strategy meeting that we had. Then I would follow-up on any inquiries. This was a real lesson for me because I learned how to sell. And I was good at it! I just enjoyed the people contact, and I think that they liked my approach, which was a soft, hard sell.

Once the prospective homebuyer arrived at one of our subdivisions, I would be at a model home and show them what was available in terms of lots and house styles. Then I would take them out and show them the lot and they would start talking about their needs… how many bedrooms, etc.

One of the first ones I worked was called Sierra Vista, southwest of town near an Army camp. I built my own beautiful custom home in one of our subdivisions, Desert Steps, I think for $28,000. It was a very attractive area of Tucson.

Flying

I operated throughout Arizona, but Arizona is a big state and we had subdivision projects all over. Consequently, in the second year I was there I went to Bob and said, "I want to fly because I'm having trouble driving to Sierra Vista to Phoenix to Flagstaff and Nogales." You just couldn't drive it. It was much easier to fly over and land. Because we had dirt strips all over the place we brought in a corporate airplane and I learned to fly.

A lot of people flew. Ted Steele was a pilot and owned a Queen Air. Several other Lusk guys, Walt Roediger and Tunis Parsons, who had been a jet jockey during Vietnam, had planes, and Raymond Ash, who was our mechanical contractor, had a particularly nice Bonanza.

Once I learned, I would fly on the company plane—I didn't have my own plane at first—for business almost daily. The company had a 180, then a 182 and then a 210. Every morning I was up and going someplace. Ted, Tunis, Walt and I flew a lot with each other. I didn't have my own plane until about five or six years later when I got to Palo Alto.

I had a lot of camaraderie with Ted Steele and Walt Roediger, and we sometimes flew recreationally, occasionally renting a plane from the company and flying down south to places like Cabo San Lucas or Guadalajara for fishing or R&R before flying home. Then we bought a boat in Mexico. Ted and I particularly did a lot of hunting together.

Helga wasn't particularly fond of all this flying around; she was scared because we had two kids and a third, Dale, was in the thought process. She was worried that I'd be careless. Engineers are good pilots because they follow the rules. People that don't follow the rules are bad pilots. She loved my friends, but she wasn't fond of me going off hunting in the south Arizona desert, flying into strips that we had never been on before.

The Lusk Approach

Bob Lusk did a very good job of promoting within. As it turned out, I loved selling, but after ten months—a long internship— he moved me up to division manager for all of Tucson. We had an insider board, which was basically the executive committee, and when I became head of the Tucson division, I also became a member of that. In my third year I joined the company's overall Board of Directors.

Soon Bob made me head of all operations in Arizona, and I eventually became president of both the

Tucson and the Arizona Homebuilders Associations and went on the board of the National Association.

Whatever my responsibility, the underlying question at Lusk was always the same: "How do you make better construction on a mass level?" Once I got out of sales and started managing ever larger operations, a group of us, including Ted Steele, Bill Baker, Walt Roediger and I, came up with a new answer, which was to do it not on site but in a plant where we could put a lot of the basic pieces together in one place without carting materials all over. This was not prefab. Prefab means you built the whole house in the plant, which was in Vail, Arizona. We just put the electrical, the plumbing and the carpentry together in the plant. That way we didn't have to deal with subcontractors, plumbers, or electricians because we got that all done at our plant. Then, instead of a load of lumber going out, we shipped out entire walls, including living rooms, kitchens, bedrooms, whatever, already electrified and plumbed, for assembly on site.

That was where engineering and design interfaced. A lot of people don't think about those things, but I like to believe that my education at three great institutions— Stanford, Harvard and MIT—had a significant impact on me.

Our approach created issues within the local building industry regarding who we were having do the carpentry, the electrical, the plumbing, and the insulation, because we didn't want to work with multiple unions and subcontractors. As was the Lusk style, we wanted to keep it in house and do it all ourselves. Fortunately, we found a precedent in a legal ruling previously handed down in a case involving United Mine Workers #128. The miners had needed to do wiring down in the mines, but electricians didn't want to go down there, so the legal ruling allowed anybody that worked digging coal in the tunnels—regardless of whether or not they were an electrician and in the electrician's union—to do the electrical work. The same ruling allowed the coal workers to become carpenters to put in the barriers, the sidewalls and the protective walls.

We used the same ruling very effectively, arguing that our plant workers could do all these different jobs, regardless of whether they were in the electrician's, plumber's, or carpenter's union. In fact, we had the carpenters do all those trades and therefore only had to deal with that one union. The carpenters, of course, were happy, but the plumbers and the electricians and other unions were upset and challenged us. We won the court case on the coal worker's precedent, but I had job threats and even death threats. I even had sugar put in my car's gas tank.

Opening California

Bob was starting to build in California, and I cautioned him about that, and particularly about the quantum leap in prices when you operate there, even in those days. But Bob was a pretty good land buyer, and we went in and started looking at land anyway. Next, he wanted me to open up California, to which I agreed, so in 1964 I moved to northern California and began to run both southern and northern California out of an office on Live Oak Avenue in Menlo Park.

Helga, the kids and I moved first moved to a rental in San Carlos, south of the City and north of Menlo Park. We knew it would be short term because we didn't yet know our long-term plans--whether we would move to Sacramento or to the Central Valley or what.

Helga was delighted to be moving back to California where Dale was born, so I made the decision that we would stay in the peninsula. After a few months I found a house

Helga and I with our young family, Dale, Ken, and Ilsi

on 89 Virginia Lane in Atherton that would be good for a family of five and called my dad. I told him I was lacking the necessary cash at that moment, but if I could just borrow about $12,000, I thought I could manage it.

We bought that house in 1964 and I paid $122,000 for it. And of course, I paid my dad back. When we sold it 28 years later in 1992, it was worth a great deal more. We raised our family there and had more fun in that house than in any other home in which we lived.

I had pretty much established myself as a builder and as the president of all these homebuilders' associations in Arizona and on the board of the national association, but I still had to get my contractor's license in California. I prepped, took and passed all the exams for the company...builders' exam, engineering exams and so on, to get the appropriate licenses. So we were legit in my side of the operation. I was really operating as a general contractor representing the Lusk Corporation developing our rapidly growing number of properties in California.

Lusk Bankruptcy

Like so many things in life, decisions are made for you. In 1967 Lusk started having financial problem and the subsequent bankruptcy was a very pivotal thing for everyone, including me.

First of all, shortly after I joined, Bob Lusk's wife filed for divorce, which created a hostile co-owner of half the company. That wasn't going to work, plain and simple, because the work hadn't been done to plan for the company's survival in this situation. In the end, Bob totally lost control of the company in the divorce; she walked away with 50% of the company and she was not friendly. That pretty well financially wrecked the company right there.

Then the company got overextended. Bob got over enthusiastic buying and developing land and then we caught the downside of a seven-year economic cycle and we couldn't get it into production. We simply built more than we could handle and couldn't sell it because of the economy. I learned a lot about the structure of the economy.

I had in fact seen this coming about six months out. The company was big and doing well but we just didn't have enough cash to weather the downturn when sales tanked. I really learned from that experience that cash is king; you simply can't have too much! The whole experience was a really great lesson in life for me.

If I had had another six months, I think I could have saved that company by getting some things underway in California, and we might not only have survived but become dominant. But we just ran out of cash.

Other people saw it happening, too, and when a company starts to hit the skids, people start calling the executives, saying, "How 'bout coming to work for me?" Lusk knew this, because everybody was doing the same thing, looking around, entertaining other offers in case Lusk went down. For instance, a company in Los Angeles called Kaufman and Broad that I knew really well wanted to hire me. I had several interviews, but said no, because I didn't want to be hired. I told them that I wanted them to buy Lusk, but that didn't fly either. Later, when I had my own business, we became friendly competitors.

In 1968, as all this was going on, Clark Oglesby came to me and said, "I want you to come and teach at Stanford." That was very pivotal, and I gave my first trial lecture at the graduate school of construction management. Apparently, it went well, and Oglesby backed me with the faculty. They brought me in as an adjunct faculty, and we agreed I'd teach two classes during the spring quarter. I was a full-fledged member of the faculty, and they were very generous, and wonderful to me: Boyd Paulson, Ray Levitts, the Fondalls, Clark all became close friends of our family.

I had really loved my seven years at Lusk. It was a great job and a fun company to be a part of, and we were paid very well. The bankruptcy taught me a lot, particularly because I had the opportunity to look at the company both as an insider and from an external perspective as president of the Tucson and Arizona Homebuilders Association. Chief among the lessons I learned was to have a very high degree of confidence in myself. I had to make decisions and believe in my own decision-making processes. I had to look at the facts and the data, project ahead, and then determine the likelihood that the data would change. Then I had to figure out my response if the data did in fact change, but always in light of my commitments etc., etc. I also had to have confidence in my ability to organize people, to get them together to seek a common goal.

Lusk helped give me that, and that was important because after the company failed, I was on my own.

RWM

Chapter Six:
My Last Regular Job and
Raising Three Great Kids (Plus a Few)
with Helga
1967—mid-1990s

Late 1960s Holistic Construction Company

In 1966, while I was teaching at Stanford, the Lusk Corporation was in the final throes of bankruptcy and it was clear it was just a matter of time before the company went under. I had all the licenses for the corporation in California, so I figured, "Why don't I just start building on my own?" I began looking to pick up some properties and bought two fairly good-sized parcels of land from Lusk on Elk Grove in Sacramento. I then built out an FHA, large-scale, affordable home development on Franklin Road. I never had a project in a tougher town with no damage whatsoever to the working site. The reason was the Police and Highway Patrol Academy was down the street from our project and there were literally hundreds of black and whites moving in the neighborhood all the time. If someone was going to mess around, they wouldn't do it there!

That was the start of my own company, which I incorporated as the Holistic Construction Company, or HCC. The name came from Helga, but I liked the term "holistic" because it encompasses the idea of whole, which describes my personal building philosophy: you build a house according to the lifestyle of the individual. I also believe that you must pay careful attention to the materials you use. That is part of Frank Lloyd Wright's utopian concept in houses, which is a very, very valid concept. I still believe in it. Our house on Miller Drive in Davis was utopian. I originally thought it was a Frank Lloyd Wright house, but then found out it was actually built by one of his protégés. But that's why I liked it so much.

While I was working at HCC, I made the most money I've ever made in my life in one transaction with a guy by the name of Tim Snow. We started with 800 units of apartments in Anaheim and converted them to condos and made a very good return on our investment. Then we used that money to buy a property in El Segundo, right near LAX. If you are flying in and look to the south, you can still see two mid-rise buildings about 16 or 17 stories high, a shopping center, and a Doubletree Hotel. Tim Snow and I did all that, and it turned out well, except we got caught in a bad market: We started the project when the vacancy factor in the El Segundo area was 2%, and when we were ready for occupancy, the vacancy percentage had rocketed to 22%. That in a nutshell reflects the vagaries of this summer.

President Nixon

During this time, I was very active in the National Association of Homebuilders. I had been active since my early days at Lusk and had been making trips back east to give some talks on building. Given that Lusk was clearly collapsing, I was also looking at the possibility of changing jobs. One day in January of 1969 I got a call from a headhunter retained by President Nixon who said he wanted to speak with me about the possibility of me being the director of the Federal Housing Administration, or FHA. That's a semi-cabinet position, and Nixon was looking at senior management guys who specialized in the operational rather than the financial side. I was a senior operations guy who was available and, unlike today when everyone is seeking diversity, I was appealing as a young, white male with significant experience in the national housing market.

I had several intensive and extensive interviews, including some very interesting one-on-ones with the president, whom I really liked. This was very heady stuff, and we got down to the point that Nixon really wanted me. Haldeman and Ehrlichman, his two henchmen whom I also got to know fairly well, didn't like me very much, or else they thought I would be competition for Nixon's attentions. I don't know. Nixon liked to play folks against each other, though, and he did it pretty well. Whatever else he was, he was one of the brightest guys I've ever met.

Naturally, Helga and I had long discussions over this, and it boiled down to the fact that we would have to move back to Washington D.C. "Honey," she said, "I really don't want to go." We talked a lot because it was a very good job. I never evaluated any job on the basis of money. I never really gave a darn about money, because it was just always there. I always seemed to get my fair share, so I never worried too much about it.

Lifestyle was the big factor. We were in our mid-thirties and living on Virginia Lane in Atherton near Helga's parents. Atherton was a beautiful town and Virginia Lane was a beautiful street and we had a tennis court, good schools and a great location. All the kids had been born in California or Arizona, I was on the faculty at Stanford, and the family was happy. We had Boy Scouts, trips to the Sierras - all those wonderful perks. It was a pretty good life. I decided that in exchange for giving up all of this, all I would gain as head of FHA was the glitter of a title, and national or international acclaim. Consequently, I finally told the President, "No, thank you."

Late 1960s: Builder's Resources Corp

About the same time, I was exploring the opportunity with the Nixon Administration, I got a call from a headhunting firm wanting to talk with me about forming a new company called Builder's Resources Corporation, which would be created out of a coalition of money from a group of companies: American Standard; National Whirlpool; Stanley Works; Donaldson, Lufkin and Jenrette; and a large real estate firm down in Los Angeles. Good companies. I really liked Stanley Works. The president, Garth Edwards, was a particularly great guy and the one with whom I had interviewed when I was at Harvard. I was intrigued because the function of the company was to raise money and then co-partner with builders in various parts of the country, which was exactly the sort of thing I was already working on. It fit into my modus operandi.

I agreed to come on as president and could develop my own projects. I spent the next four or five years building that company up. Early on I hired a guy by the name of Dick Little to be my number two. Dick became a longtime friend of mine. One of the first firms we partnered with was Miller and Smith, run by my old Harvard Business School classmates. That was a nice tie. We invested in a lot of these projects and did well with them.

Third Creek

I also connected with my old friend from Stanford, Dick Balch, who had hired me at MIT when I was at Harvard Business School. Balch knew the Waggenheim family, which owned Granny Goose Potato Chip Company, was looking for some help on a real estate project and he recommended me. Mervyn Waggenheim then got in touch with me about some land he wanted to develop in Incline Village in Reno. Naturally, I said, "Sure, that's the kind of development that I'm pretty good at doing."

I came on as an adviser, and we named the development Third Creek. We got a huge loan from Toronto Dominion Bank, a Canadian Bank, and I got the zoning approved and started working on the houses. As I was working on the zoning and planning, Waggenheim took his whole management team on a plane ride, using a Queen Air, to ski at Sun Valley. On the return, their pilot thought he could make it all the way back to Marin without gassing up, but he was wrong, and the plane crashed in the Marin foothills, and wiped out the whole group. Six guys! That was a real blow. I couldn't believe how stupid and careless that pilot was, because I myself was flying a lot then and recognized the carelessness of that decision.

Soon thereafter, Mrs. Waggenheim called me up and asked me to take over the project and finish it. Partially because I was feeling so sympathetic toward her and wanted to try to help her out, and partially because Dick Balch encouraged me to, I said yes, which was one of the only fatal business decisions I have ever made. I should have said no and told her that I didn't have the time or the inclination. I was just an adviser, and it was going to take too much of my time and energy to actually take it over and run it on a day-to-day basis. Long story short, Third Creek got hit by the downturn in the building industry; the interest rates went way up and carrying that loan from the bank in Toronto was difficult, if not impossible. Eventually we let it go.

On the upside, I had built a unit in there that we had for about ten years, so that was fun. Helga spent three solid months up there writing her doctoral thesis for the California Institute of Transpersonal Psychology. She always said she couldn't have done it without the peace and quiet and the solitude of Third Creek.

At Builder's Resources we got ourselves in a mess like Third Creek in a couple of situations, but we always worked our way out of them. We had a good board, made up of members from each of the companies, so I was dealing with really bright people. As much as I liked Garth Edwards at Stanley Tools, I found Harold Geneen at AT&T to be, shall we say, more than difficult—a characteristic which comes through in his autobiography. I used to fly into New York, and they would helicopter me over to the building. Then he made me wait. He thought he was a king; I found him very unlikeable.

There was one sticking point in the whole deal from the beginning, and it helped hasten the end: they wanted me to relocate to Southern California. I refused, and they didn't like that. The chairman of the board, who was the head of the real estate firm in L.A., was difficult to work with at best. He was the one who was constantly putting pressure on me to move to L.A. He was a pretty arrogant guy who wanted me under his thumb, and I wouldn't do that. Instead, I'd fly down all the time to the L.A. office, until eventually I said the heck with it. It didn't matter where we were located. It really didn't, so I based the company out of the office I already had on Live Oak, in Menlo Park, and moved all the L.A. guys up to northern California. But I was constantly in a tug of war over this issue.

After about three years of this I said I was just plain not happy and departed. When I finally decided I was through with it, I went to a couple of the owners and told them that I wasn't happy, that I didn't really like answering to people like Geneen and the chairman. I told them I was better than that and that I was not the man for them and that I was going to leave.

The good thing was that I was vested; I had smartly negotiated a deal up front that said if things didn't work out, I had the right to sell the company. Shortly after I had announced my intention to depart, I was in New York on a panel talking to a convention of builders. As I was speaking, somebody brought a note up from a gentleman named Maersk Moller; the note said he wanted

to speak with me after the panel discussion. I asked Bob
Rice, who was Senior VP of Citicorp Real Estate and
sitting next to me on the panel, if he knew who Maersk
Moller was. He said, "Bob, that guy is one of the
wealthiest men in world, and if he wants to see you, go
see him." He was right. Maersk Moller owned the Maersk
Lines—you see the name on shipping containers all over
the world. They also owned Scandinavian Airways,
among many other companies, and real estate
everywhere.

I jotted a note back that said I would be happy to
meet with him, and another note came back which said,
"After your talk give me a call and we'll get together for
coffee."

As it turned out, Maersk looked exactly like my
father: same complexion, same reddish hair, beautiful
blue eyes and a goatee. He told me he had been watching
Builder's Resources, and wanted to buy us as his real
estate wing in Europe and the U.S. That turned out to be
a very interesting and enjoyable time, because Helga and I
had a couple of very nice trips to Europe, mainly
Denmark and Norway, during our discussions. Maersk
wanted to have me with the deal, but I said, "No, I'm not
going to be part of it. I'm going to go off on my own." I
didn't want to work in Europe. But we sold Builder's
Resources to Maersk, and Maersk used the new group as
its real estate wing in Europe. The Board loved the deal
because they weren't really happy with the company in
the first place; the returns were just not there at the levels
they had hoped. By selling it, though, we made them all
happy.

Builder's Resources had been a useful step for me,
even though I didn't always enjoy it. I had started the

company and gotten it going. I had learned a lot about corporate America and hired some really good people. It was probably the first job I had ever lost interest in, though. After several years I was just ready to move on, and it turned out to be the last formal job I had working as an employee for somebody else.

The Kids

Through all of this, of course, Helga and I were raising Ken, Ilsi and Dale, who are very different individuals.

Ken, our oldest, was always very independent and extraordinarily competent. After high school he went to Whitman College to study physics and geology, then pursued graduate studies in geology at Kansas State and San Diego State, and eventually came back to Stanford to get his master's degree in civil engineering.

Ken's a prolific reader who has taught himself a great deal in fields in which he's interested. He was always studying something! He can tear just about anything apart and put it back together again faster than anybody I've ever seen. He's a very good engineer. Around the house, he does all the work himself, and fixes the plumbing and the electricity. He's remodeled his own kitchen and bathrooms in several houses and is an expert chef who does all the

Ken during his high school years

cooking in his household. He's a bright, capable guy— a doer—and he has an enormous amount of energy.

He is married to Sarah Hokanson, and with her has a son Robert Allan, named after his two grandfathers, who is a recent graduate of Stonybrook University. He is currently in the Army Special Forces training program.

Dale is totally different from his big brother. He is the most sensitive of the three children. Dale has always been lucky—it seems like he has two lucky genies sitting on his shoulders guiding him through this morass we call life. He has fun and enjoys things and is one of the most well-liked persons I've ever known. Everybody likes Dale and enjoys his glowing outlook on life. That is the way he plays his sports, that is the way he

Dale in his usual soccer uniform

went to school, and that is the way he is with his own kids. He is just out there. He is a wonderful guy to be around. Dale is the lucky guy whose instincts are always right on.

After high school, he played soccer at the University of Redlands. In 1988, after graduate school at the University of Pennsylvania, Dale worked at the U.S. Environmental Protection Agency's Office of International Affairs. In 1994, he applied for a fellowship from the Alexander von Humboldt Foundation. With that, he lived in Bonn, Germany, and worked at the German Environment Ministry and an environmental think tank. He also had the chance to play amateur soccer.

It was shortly after Dale's time in Bonn that he met his future wife, Amy Houpt, an economist and cellist. In

2007, Dale received his doctorate at Virginia Tech in environmental planning, where his research focused on the transfer and application of German urban environmental policy innovations to U.S. cities. In 2010, Dale returned to Germany again as a fellow of the Alexander von Humboldt Foundation, to undertake further research at the Free University of Berlin on the transfer of German energy innovations to U.S. cities. Dale continues to stay active with U.S.-German relations and cultural, science and academic organizations.

Dale and Amy have raised three children – Eliza (born 2001) and twin sisters Mia and Victoria (born 2004). Amy passed along her musical abilities to all three, now high-school age daughters: Eliza, Mia and Tori play the viola, the guitar and the cello respectively.

Ilsi is one of the most present persons I've ever met in my life. She is an astute observer. She is an incredibly hard working, think-it-though person, particularly on the details, and smoothly masters all the processes, practices and procedures. The bottom line is: Ilsi knows how to get stuff done.

Ilsi is her mother's daughter!

She's also the opposite of me in many ways. I'm impatient; she's patient. I'm provocative; she's cooperative. I'm in your face; she surrounds you with love. She pretty much picked all that up from her mother, Helga. Of the three, she's the most like Helga—the spitting image of her mother, and a remarkable young lady.

Ilsi grew up riding and caring for horses, and thus knew what she wanted from day one. She went to Pomona College, then to Cornell to study pre-veterinary medicine, and then came back UC Davis for her veterinarian's degree. She received honors all the way through, from high school through Cornell to Davis.

Today she is a skilled and progressive veterinarian who combines standard western medical practices with eastern acupuncture and acupressure. She is ahead of the curve and excels in whatever she pursues.

Helga and I hiking in the Trinity Alps in Northern California

Along with her husband, Dr. Clare Gregory, Ilsi is my principal caregiver. They both are extraordinarily competent, as they are at all things that they do, and devoted. I depend a great deal not only on their care but on their presence and am profoundly grateful to them both.

Both Dale and Ken are Eagle scouts. All three kids have traveled with us overseas and hiking in the California Sierras and Himalayas.

We also sort of unofficially adopted other kids, usually Stanford students, throughout the years. I don't know when that started, but it was something we did. We had big house and we had room, and in our grand scheme of things, we always thought it would be nice to have people in to help us out. We wouldn't charge them anything and if they came in and stayed…they could babysit and help out around the house in exchange for rent. A good deal for everyone. Horst Koeppen, who was from Germany, actually became kind of our fourth child. He lived with us for years and became like a brother to the other three. I am still very close to Horst and have visited him from time to time in Germany, where he now lives.

I always told these "extra" kids that if they stayed with us, there would be chores to do. That was the idea. They were part of the family, so there were chores: there is grass to cut and leaves to rake and trimming to do. These were life lessons. The truth is that I loved working outdoors, and I was the one guy in our household that would take care of the yard.

All the kids worked for me at one time or another. I had them clean out the gardens or working at Third Creek. Ilsi, of course, was always working with the horses in Portola Valley or Woodside. She moved around a little

bit with the horses, but she was always involved with equestrian activities, and always had her own horse.

The kids and I on vacation

We never had any significant challenges with the kids. The closest to that would have been Ken when he went off on his own. But they were all independent self-starters. That is more a trait of mine than Helga's. But if there was a family or parenting debate, Helga always won. I eventually learned that her decision was almost always the right one, even though I never wanted to admit it.

For me, parenting was made easier because I was home a lot. On the other hand, I guess I also travelled probably more that I should have, and I wasn't home on a lot of key things. I think I was a relatively good father, but you'd have to ask our children about that. What was Dad good at and what was he bad at? But we had three very different kids who ended up incredibly well educated at a variety of different schools. Helga, Ilsi and Dale have their doctorates and Ken has two masters'. We had our challenges, like any family, but we also had a lot of fun, I love and enjoy all three of the kids equally and enormously.

Trips

We traveled a lot as a during the years that the kids were growing up - the late 1960s, 1970s, and early 1980s. Helga would always plan our trips when we traveled as a group. We'd take friends backpacking up in the Sierras or on 50 milers with the Boy Scouts. We were always doing that.

Visiting in Germany with Horst Koeppen, one of the many students who lived with us while going to school, and perhaps the one with whom we remained closest throughout our lives.

The boys were into scouting, and Ilsi was doing her horseback riding, but she was also a terrific hiker— absolutely terrific. She and Helga bonded on that, and I bonded with the boys on scouting. Each of the children and Horst have been with us to Nepal, and all are very talented hikers and experienced campers and travelers.

Family ski trip in Park City, Utah

The Boy Scouts were wonderful. As a young man I wasn't really a scout for very long in Kansas City. Where are you going to hike in Kansas City—along the Missouri River? My eyes to scouting opened up when I came out to California and got into the Sierras. That is just spectacular....just like I'd remembered from our family trip when I was four.

Generally, we spent a lot of time with the kids. We hiked, we skied, and spent a lot of time in the outdoors. As a family we used to ski a lot with Dick Little, who worked with me at Builder's Resources, and his family. Our wives and kids got along well. Early on we used the condo I had built up at Third Creek, but eventually the kids said they were tired of skiing Tahoe and wanted to go to Park City, Vail and Sun Valley and to ski other wonderful new spots. These places are far away, so we sold the place at Third Creek and started flying to Colorado. We had more fun both in

On the way to Sun River with the kids, Dales' wife, Amy, Kenny's wife, Sarah, and Helga's mom, Hilde

Third Creek and in Colorado and anywhere we went as a family. Of course, flying is very dangerous, so I'm glad we never had a problem. I lost a lot of good friends flying. It breaks me up to think of them.

It was about 1978 that we started going to Nepal. The first trip was totally on a lark, because I was joining the board of Geographic Travel and Expeditions, Inc., a company which had started in the Himalayas in 1981 when a small group of about 15 Americans became one of the first outside groups allowed to hike into the Tibetan backcountry. Subsequent to that first trip, one of the group, Jo Sanders, founded a company she called InnerAsia, an adventure travel company to the newly opened Tibet and China.

Not long after, George Doubleday, an experienced adventure traveler, formed a company, Geographic Travel

My 70th birthday party with my brothers and their families

and Expeditions, and asked me to join the board along with a friend of his, Al Read. I encouraged George, who had been a Marine pilot in Vietnam, when I arranged my own trips through them to the Galapagos, Turkey and later, Nepal. George brought a lot of people onto the board, including me and changed the name to Geographic Expeditions, or GeoEx for short, and it became a leading adventure travel company.

I met Al Read on one of the Nepal trips. He had been one of America's great climbers and was stationed with the State Department in Nepal. We talked and he said he'd like to get involved in starting a company that was a purveyor of exotic travel in various parts of the world. So Al joined, and GeoEx then started to engage in more unusual and challenging areas of exploration.

My family went hiking and camping in Nepal with GeoEx about every two years between 1979 and 1986. Our friends the Enthovens joined us on the trips to Turkey, then the Galapagos, and finally to Nepal. It was on these trips where we met Patricia Demetrius who was a very attractive woman and a classmate of Helga's at the Institute of Transpersonal Psychology, where, like Helga, she earned her doctorate. Pat owned Marine Land USA, a dolphin sanctuary in California. She was a good friend.

In the early 2000s Helga and I went to Uruguay for the wedding of one of the kids who lived with us while he was going to school, Rafael Ruano. There were actually four Ruanos who went to Stanford between about 1965 and 2000, and they were all business managers of the basketball team at different times. It was a family tradition. Their father was one of my first students.

Before we got to Uruguay, we stopped to visit Iquazu Falls in Argentina, near the border with Brazil. Unfortunately, during this first stage of the trip, Helga had her purse stolen right off of her arm. She knew it within 15 seconds, but the thieves were long gone. The next day we had to go through cancelling credit cards and all the other aggravation related to having your documents stolen. Bank of America, though, wouldn't take an international phone call, and by the time I called Ken minutes after we realized it had been stolen, and he got it cancelled, the thieves had already started charging on it. Had Bank of America accepted the call like American Express did, they could have caught the guy in the act.

I was most worried, of course, about Helga's passport, but the embassy told us thieves didn't like to get caught with a passport, and for kind of a silly reason. The tradition is that they were guilty of a sin if they dumped it in a trashcan and it was never found, but if it's found, they were not guilty anymore. Now there's a world class' rationalization! That tradition led in Argentina to leaving the passports in the city cemetery. You only lose your cards and always get your passports and IDs back.

The Uruguayan authorities told us that Helga's passport would almost certainly be at the cemetery on the other side of the wall from such and such a location the next morning, which was apparently the standard, agreed-upon dumping spot for stolen passports to be recovered. Sure enough, the next morning there were about 25 passports over there, Helga's included. The police dutifully handed them back to all of us assembled tourists who had had them stolen the day before. It was pretty funny but also a great relief.

Between long hiking trips in the Sierra Nevadas, scouts, equestrian events, skiing with friends at Tahoe and Colorado, and more exotic trips to places like Nepal, we had an immense amount of fun as a family. Those times with Helga and the kids are some of my fondest memories.

RWM

Chapter Seven
After Builder's Resources:
Silicon Valley Bank and Various
Directorships

The First of Many Directorships

Once I was free of Builder's Resources in the early 1970s and truly on my own, I became really interested in directorships. From that point forward, I was always on about three or four boards which allowed me to continue my strategy of providing ample income to continue to live comfortably.

My first directorship had been with the Lusk Corporation, starting in 1964. That was a good board to learn from because I also served on the executive committee. It was timely, and I was in operations, so this had a powerful influence on me.

The second was Wilsey and Ham, a local civil engineering firm. Lee Ham was a wonderful engineer and built an excellent firm in San Mateo, serving northern California. I was his first outside board member and that put me back in the profession which I dearly loved. The thing that was especially good about that job was that it allowed me to have an office right in Foster City, California.

Unfortunately, Lee wanted to build new towns and large, planned commercial developments offshore. I said, "Lee, you don't want to do that, as we have plenty of opportunities here. You really want to focus on these new towns here, like Foster City and elsewhere in the area." But he wanted to go offshore. I continued to say, "No way! First," I argued, "your health is declining. Number two, you would be dealing with foreign governments and foreign currencies. And third, we don't have the temperament or the financial resources to do something like that. You don't want to do it...it'll be a mess."

That battle on the board over this went on and on. Finally, I was going to leave, but some of the board members who shared my views wanted me to stay with the company. That was a real conflict, because I respected Lee and I really didn't want to anger him to that extent. So I talked to a lot of the employees, and then Lee appointed me chairman of Wilsey and Ham. I ran the company briefly, but then we hired a terrific engineer, Bill Kull, to run the company.

Eventually, Bill and I and a couple of the independent engineers and investors bought half the company. We split from the other half and called our company WH Pacific. We kept the name because it was valuable. We didn't change the format whatsoever, just the ownership. The new company was headquartered in Bellevue, Washington and we had three very capable engineers named Jeff Dagget in Seattle, Bill Jabs in Portland and Tom Williams in Bend, Oregon, who ran the principal offices and were the key partners who developed the company. The market was anybody who needed civil engineering. We did small airports, such as the one in Eugene, Oregon and civil engineering projects in the four states of Washington, Alaska, Oregon, and Idaho.

After building it up WH Pacific's profitability and acquiring other companies in Alaska, we sold WH Pacific to an engineering firm in the UK. Bill Kull and I remained lifetime friends after the sale and remain so to this day.

Silicon Valley Bank

With my courses going well at Stanford, I continued to have more and more involvement with startups and directorships. I had some involvements with venture capitalists, and as I looked around, I began to realize that venture capital was having a problem with second-round financing. In short, the entrepreneurs were coming back to venture capitalists, who had initially funded them, for second-round financing. The VCs hated that because second-round financing, by its very nature, diluted their positions. The spurned entrepreneurs then had to go further afield to raise more money. It seemed to me that that was a bank's function, but the banks weren't doing it either, because they did not understand the start-up business model. They just did not want any more risk.

One of my former students, Hernan Martinez of Argentina, was involved in the banking side of venture capital. Hernan was a really bright guy who had gone to work for a Southern California financial institution, and he was doing something different with venture capital and second-round financing, so I visited him to learn what he was doing.

Eventually I wrote a paper about how to structure second-round venture capital financing, and from that exercise, I determined that I could start a bank that would do the second-round financing that VCs wouldn't and that was too risky for traditional banks.

I had two safeguards, and they were very simple. First, the management team had already been approved by the venture capitalists, who generally do a very good job of that. Because the VCs had vetted both the concept and the entrepreneurs themselves, our risk was substantially reduced. With a very rigorous due diligence already done, it was easy for us to invest in the entrepreneurs.

Second, I wanted the venture capitalists to make deposits in our bank. Fortunately, this was not only easy for them to do, but it made a lot of sense. Banks rely on deposits, not profits, for growth. Profits are necessary to get the deposits, but if you have the appropriate relationships, you can get the deposits while you are growing in profitability. I wanted the VCs to make their deposits at my bank because they were making a lot of money.

From the VC's perspective, there were several benefits. First, our bank was willing to pay a higher interest rate than the banks for their money, thus we provided an attractive parking place for their money. Secondly, and even more importantly, we were going to offer the second-round financing without taking any positions in the companies (although the bank began to do that years later, after I left). Consequently, our backing would not deplete the VC's stakes. That had been the big hurdle. Finally, by investing in the companies they had backed initially, we were supporting their initial investment with our own.

We were private and started with five million dollars. I was the chairman and acting chief executive officer. Early on we hired Roger Smith to be our president. Roger had been senior vice president at Wells Fargo and had strong relationships within the VC community throughout Silicon Valley. We also brought on Laurie Saporito, who had been a corporate secretary of another start-up bank, as our corporate secretary. We positioned ourselves as specialists in second-round financing of start-up companies, and we were good at it because we had very strong relationships with the entire community through Bill and Roger's work. We made some commercial loans, but we didn't do any real estate. I knew real estate, but the others didn't, and I wanted us to stick with what we knew within the banking sector.

Silicon Valley Bank hit the marketplace like a roaring fire. The VCs loved it. They just flocked to the bank and stuck in those deposits, and we grew quickly. Kleiner Perkins was an investor with us. Sutter Hill Capital, and specifically Paul Wise, their president, was wonderful. Paul saw our vision and made an early commitment to invest, which was of great help.

The Myth of the Poker Game

One somewhat humorous story about the bank was that it had its beginning at a poker game. This story circulated around the Valley for years. That was Bill Biggerstaff's malarkey. Bill was a very close friend of mine who had worked his whole life in banking. He was a hearty fellow, well educated...a big smiling teddy bear. He welcomed the start-up project, so I hired him as a sort of public affairs guy. His job was to build on his many connections and introduce Silicon Valley Bank to the community, and he did an excellent job of that over the years.

About the same time I hired Bill, a poker group had started when Burton Blackwell, a neighbor and close friend of mine, and I struck up a discussion while we were skiing in Park City. I said, "You know, Burton, you and I know a lot of people. Let's start a poker game. That would be really fun. Low stakes poker. Nobody is going to get hurt."

The initial group was Burton, Biggerstaff, Jack Butler, Dave Elliott, Starr Colby, who worked for Lockheed, Bob Proctor, Fred Rehmus and me. All close friends from Atherton. This group played poker once a month on Friday nights, rotating venues between our homes. The host provided the dinner. Some of us cooked it on our own and some of us had significant help from our wives.

It was a very compatible group of men, and we had much fun. We went for a long time—15 or 20 years—and we were really known around town as the poker group. Every spring we would rent a couple of houses and take the families down to Pajero Dunes. The men would go down Friday, cook dinner and play poker all night. Then the families and kids would come down Saturday morning and we would stay through Sunday night.

Now, Biggerstaff always inhabited the gray area between truth and exaggeration, but not in a bad or scheming way. He just had a tendency to gild the lily a bit—it was part of his charm—and he thought it would make a good story to plant the inception of the bank in the poker game.

We had in fact talked to Dave Elliott, who was a fellow ATO with me at Stanford, two years my senior, an adviser throughout my life, and a dear friend whose family and ours shared many a pleasant time together. We told Dave we were starting a bank and asked him his thoughts on it...as we continued to do for years. That was common in the poker group; we'd typically have two or three beers, play poker and discuss the week's or month's activity. But other than these offhand discussions, the poker group had nothing to do with the startup of Silicon Valley Bank other than serving as a sounding board. But Biggerstaff liked to pass that story on about the origin of it all and it became the talk of the Valley. It sounded like an interesting hook to him...and it does make a good story.

More Directorships: RMS and PAMA

In about 1993, Silicon Valley Bank filed the papers for an initial public offering. It also planned to start issuing first-round financing in which it would take positions in start-ups. At that point I said, "I'm out." I had established a rule at the bank that required senior officers, presidents, CEOs, and chairmen to leave after serving ten years, and mine were about up anyway. I had done what I wanted to do: I'd formed the bank, and it was operating successfully under Roger Smith's guidance. I enjoyed that start-up immensely and stayed on the board until it was successfully under operation.

Silicon Valley Bank was clearly the most important company I started because it was the first one. It was

incredibly successful, and it proved to me that my
intuitive skills and thought processes were fairly good.
From that whole experience I learned that I had the most
fun starting these companies and getting them
operational, but that I didn't care about the operational
development after I'd gotten them up and running. I just
really wanted to start them. That is what I was good at. I
could see an idea, I could wrestle with it, mature it and
then put it out to grow.

Ultimately, I found I was best at just being on
boards. I just enjoyed it. So from then on, I primarily
concentrated on directorships. Some of them did require
some hands-on activity, though. If the president or
somebody in the organization wanted my day-to-day help
in some particular area, I was happy to contribute as an
advisor.

After Silicon Valley Bank, my second company was
called Risk Management Software (RMS). The genius
behind that company was a student of mine, Hemant
Shah, whose father was Professor Haresh Shah, the chair
of civil engineering department at Stanford. Helmet wrote
a report on risk management and gave it to me as part of
the requirements of my class. I was greatly impressed with
the it, went to Haresh and said, "You know your son was
in my class, and he has written this paper. By golly, the
concept is really great! You guys ought to start this
company! It's a very sound opportunity."

There was always a lot of statistical data on risk,
specifically earthquake risk. For instance, earthquake risk
analysis for a building would factor in the year that a
building was built, the building code at the time, and its
proximity to the nearest earthquake. Risk Management
Software then developed a statistical model for

earthquake probability and consequences based on these algorithms in order to analyze the risk for the purposes of insurance-based investment. RMS would predict what kind of damage a particular building would sustain given an earthquake intensity of 7.5, or whatever, on the Richter scale. Interested parties could then use this assessment in their analysis of the economic uncertainties of their project.

Everybody needs that analysis. Certainly, the insurance company, but also the owner, mortgage companies, the government. Everybody! So, the market for earthquake risk analysis is basically a multitude of parties of interest...lenders, owners, insurers, etc. The company would approach, for example, Bank of America, and say, "You need this product for all your buildings, because you've been paying the same rate across the board for earthquake insurance. That's problematic because one building, built in a relatively stable area under more recent and more stringent buildings codes, has a far different exposure to risk than an older building sitting on top of the San Andreas Fault. There is no comparison between the two, and RMS could quantify each building's risk profile.

Nothing like that had existed before. Until RMS came along, the insurance industry had no basis to evaluate how much insurance was needed or what the risk for a particular building might be. They were operating on what I would call an aggregated assault on the integrity of pragmatic reasoning. So, I told Haresh that it was a big market, and we should start the company. So, we got together over a series of weekends and developed the company.

As a founder and a board member, my role was conceptualizing. I stayed with them for three or four years while they got it going. Hemant Shah, who had written the report in my class, was the start-up president. Risk Management Solutions (RMS) was a big success. Now they are international with offices all over the world, and they undertake disaster analysis and assess risk related to water, rain, typhoons, hurricanes.... all kinds of natural events.

PAMA

In the 1980s I settled in teaching at Stanford, working with the bank, and finding more opportunities to serve as a corporate director. Life was good, but I really wanted to do some building, because that was always my first love. Fortunately, an opportunity existed with some properties in Sacramento County I had purchased from Lusk in that company's final years. I began building houses on that property.

Next, I formed an LLC with yet another former student, Mark Cunningham, who was a builder in Sacramento. His company was called PAMA, an acronym of his wife, Pat, and his first names. I was asked to be on the board and helped raise money and guide the company for what turned out to be about seven or eight years. We built houses, apartments, and condominiums. Pretty much everything. Our production manager was another former student of mine from Stanford, Raphael Ruano. Raphael was a bright, hard-working guy from Uruguay, in South America, and a superb construction manager.

Even though I was just a board member, it took a lot of my time because we were in constant meetings buying land, selling land, negotiating, and getting money. I focused principally on financing, but we worked together for the next ten years until Mark and I both retired.

Helga

Through everything I was doing, Helga was very active on a peripheral basis. She was not active in the business directly, but she was supportive, and she served as a vital sounding board on everything that I did.

Morning was always our time of talking and planning. It was a time of reflection. I'd get up and read my *Wall Street Journal* and have my Frappuccino and an early breakfast, then she would come out and we would talk about what we had planned for the day.

Soon, we'd go off on some current subject in the paper. These talks were deeper...we'd talk about how we really felt about this or that, maybe who we were going to back in an election. We didn't fill out ballots together, but we talked about all the propositions. How are you voting on this and why, and so on? We were pretty much aligned most of the time, however she was more liberal than I am, and often made me see the light, particularly when I did not want to.

Helga was the dominant thinker, the king and the queen and the chief clerk. Even though she left the business side to me, her judgement was solid as a rock, and she was incredibly street-smart, in addition to her academic brilliance. She weighed in on things, and she was just a terrific observer of people. She got that intuitive part from her dad, but she also had a lot of experience from her nursing, her doctoral work, her work at the hospital, and from raising the kids. Kids are great teachers. Generally speaking, the mistakes I made came when I didn't follow Helga's advice. She was and still is in many ways my strategic partner. I still ask Helga, "What would you do in this situation?" Though she passed away three years ago, she was the principal partner in my life and remains so to this day. Her spiritual presence is still with me. She of all people had the greatest impact on my life, and I miss her greatly.

Move to Davis

I closed out my career in directorships with PAMA and retired when I was 75, when Helga and I moved permanently to Davis.

Reflecting on these ventures also gives me the chance to thank a book group that Helga and I belonged to during these twilight times. This group was Jim and Lynn Gibbons, Theda and Oscar Firschein, Tom and Nancy Fiene, and Wendy and Masoon Wilrich. We were together over a 40-year period, during which time we met about five times a year to discuss books, principally novels. This was a huge growing period for me, which, upon reflection, was invaluable, and I am so indebted to those nine for their nurturing and for educating me.

RWM

Chapter Eight:
Russia & Georgia, 1986-2005

Russia

In 1986, before I left the bank, I got a phone call from a guy named Abel Aganbegyan, who was essentially the Paul Voelker, or Federal Reserve Chairman, of the Soviet Union. Aganbegyan was a big guy, with a cabinet level position in the Communist party. I had no clue who he was, but he had looked me up because I had started the bank and my name was all over the SEC application. He knew that the bank was successful after four years of operation, and he wanted to find out if they could do it in Russia.

I immediately told him that there was no way in Sam Hill they could do it, because of the nature of the Russian political and economic system, but he wanted to come out and talk with me anyway. What ensued turned out to be a very interesting conversation that lasted basically the rest of my career.

The meeting with Aganbegyan also reignited my relationship with George Shultz, whom I had met before through his involvement with the Hoover Institution at

Stanford. When Aganbegyan called, I realized I didn't know anything about Russia and needed the advice of someone who did, so before the Hilton meeting, I called George, who was retired from the government at this point.

My favorite story about George Shultz emerged from our first meeting.

Shultz had five chairs, each of which corresponded to the senior government posts he had held: secretary of labor, treasury, state, director of the Office of Management and Budget and so on. When I arrived, he said "Mr. Medearis, it's nice to have you here. Who would you like to be today? I'll be Secretary of State." I picked a cabinet post and he said, "There is your chair."

I told him about Aganbegyan's call, and George said he was willing to be helpful. When he said, "Let's do something about it," it was clear that he thought this might be a unique opportunity for the country. "The first thing you do," he went on, "is that you do it! Meet with him." He laid no ground rules down whatsoever, but he wanted me to keep him posted. So I said I would do that. My understanding of what I was walking into was much better with Shultz briefing me and we developed a relationship which was really quite strong.

That's also the first time I met Hedrick Smith, the journalist who focused on Russia, who heard I was going to be with Aganbegyan and contacted me to say he said he'd like to know more about our meeting. Hedrick was a very bright guy, and we had several interviews over the ensuing years as I brought him up to date as events unfolded.

The Meeting

My first meeting with Abel Aganbegyan took place at the Airport Hilton at SFO. I told him that I couldn't explain to him what we did at the bank. Instead, I'd have to show him. I had already called Roger Smith, our president, and said, "I'm going to bring this guy down to the bank. I'd like to show him a couple of things that we do. The kinds of loans we make and so on."

I told Abel that we'd go to Silicon Valley and then have dinner at my house. He changed his schedule for all this, but he was still an hour late. The Russians have no sense of time; time just means nothing to them. I thought, "Boy, if we ever get in a war with these guys, we'll kick their ass." They just have no concept of being on time or organizing things.

Once he came down, we met for about three hours at the Hilton. It was a very engaging conversation, though it stayed strictly to the economics of the banking industry, and nothing else. Like his boss, Gorbachev, Aganbegyan spoke fluent English.

After our meeting we got in my car to go visit the companies Bill Biggerstaff had lined up for us to see. I knew two of them, but Bill knew where they were, so we picked him up on the way. Aganbegyan, by the way, was a very big man, about 6'8" and probably 400 pounds. When he got in my car, the hydraulics went "pffffffftt," and the car sank and settled very close to the pavement.

We visited two companies before we were pulled over by a whole string of police cars. When the officer came to my window, he said, "We've been following you, Mr. Medearis."

"I see that," I said.

Then it hit me. I knew what this was about! The Russians could visit San Mateo, but not Silicon Valley. Aganbegyan was a pretty important guy, and they were watching him when I picked him up, and they just followed us. So I invited the cops to come with me. I said, "I don't know how to address this, but why don't you just come along? This guy [meaning Aganbegyan] is innocent. I don't have a camera with me, so I'm not taking pictures and I won't let them take pictures, etc."

We went on with police escort from the Highway Patrol, and I'm sure they were interspersed with agents.

On Malcolm Forbes' jet, the Capitalist Tool, along with Jim Garrison

They let us visit some clean rooms.

Aganbegyan and his whole entourage— there were four or five Russians with him, half of whom I'm sure were KGB—ended up going to dinner at my house, which at this point was a condominium on Bryant Street in Palo Alto, and it was a very interesting evening. Unfortunately, the dinner part was a disaster, at least from Helga's perspective. She had fixed a beautiful meal of roast lamb with all the fixings, but by this time we were hours late and the food was all cold. Helga was just beside herself. I said, "Honey, you've just got to go with the flow. Forget about it." The dinner was wonderful, but I felt so sorry for Helga because she's a perfectionist.

I had some great wines available, but they didn't want wine. They wanted American bourbon! We were of course in wine country, very far away from Kentucky, but they still wanted bourbon. These guys were real drinkers. I had made a rule that whenever I was going to get involved in foreign affairs, I wouldn't drink, so I told them I was an alcoholic, and if I started drinking, I could go on a binge. It was all B.S., but I had to say I didn't drink and mean it. These guys would drink me under the table...they'd have me seven sheets under. The whole situation was unreal. I'll never forget it.

The next day I had us lined up to go to Esalen, which took a lot of guts, I guess, because Esalen was new age retreat center and also a free form think tank where things can get done without restrictions. Fortunately, the founder and head of Esalen, Michael Murphy and his wife Dolse, both spoke fluent Russian. Anyway, we all ended up naked in the hot tub, which is huge, about half the size of average living room. It held 40 people and sat in beautiful surroundings overlooking the Pacific Ocean north of Big Sur and south of Carmel. The flowers were just gorgeous. Helga went down there almost every year to get re-aligned.

We all stayed the night and had a great time, and the Russians were just watching the whole time. You know, when men and women are in the hot tub together and they are having a glass of wine...well, you get really juiced up with alcohol in a hot tub. But watching the sunset over the Pacific, there is quality to the interaction unlike other situations. That trip to Esalen was a real eye opener.

"This is a guy I can work with," I thought of Aganbegyan after two days, but ultimately, I just kept telling him that you can't replicate Silicon Valley Bank in a communist country because the state can take over at any time. In communism, in which no one owns any assets, I asked him "how can I as a banker require securitization of loans? I've got to have some asset basis; I've got to have security." That was my first point: in a communist system, the necessary collateral is not possible because no one owns anything.

"Number two," I said, "you're a dictatorship. You can step in, take over and run things any time you want to. No one's going to have a bank like Silicon Valley if you have that as a fundamental undercarriage of your lending policy.

"And the third thing," I said bluntly, "is that you have a culture of corruption."

These guys were surprised that they were being talked to that way. In the end, though, Aganbegyan said, "Mr. Medearis, would you come to Russia and tell the board that?" By that he meant the board of Communist Council, which is like our president's cabinet.

I said, "If you meet my terms, and you pay me what I need, the answer is yes."

Travel

A month and a half later I was on the first of many trips to Russia. In Moscow I stayed in a hotel that is actually in the Kremlin. Of course, I had an interpreter who was a KGB guy, which I expected because Shultz had told me that that it was the way things go over there, and to go with it the best I could. You're never by yourself in Russia, because everything is bugged. Shultz gave me a great briefing on all this stuff.

Aganbegyan wanted me to tell Gorbachev what I'd told him, so I met with Gorbachev and the Communist Council at Gorbachev's office in the Kremlin. For them I was an interesting private contact because I had no governmental ties whatsoever. But they knew I'd had been in the service and what I did there; they probably knew more about me than I know about myself.

In the meeting we had interpreters who wanted us to speak in Russian, but Gorbachev violated all that protocol. I'd speak in English and the interpreter would translate, and Gorbachev would respond in English. Gorbachev's English is excellent.

I went through the three principles again, and Gorbachev got up from behind his desk, came around and said, "Mr. Medearis, we needed to hear that. You are absolutely right. I'll work on that."

And Gorbachev did work on it. He said, "We've got to change this system…it's not working." Although a lot of people didn't realize it, these guys knew they were in big trouble because the Russian economy was so deeply in the tank it could cause the USSR to fall.

In addition to speaking with him and the Council, Gorbachev wanted me to teach a class on pragmatic western capitalism. He would orchestrate this whole thing from the Kremlin, and he wanted the classes to be given to specific students that the Party had chosen. These students were apparatchiks – party functionaries who were going to be going to work in western embassies and other similar positions. Gorbachev and the Council wanted these people to have an understanding of things in the countries they would be working and visiting.

I ended up teaching a series of classes out at Vladimir, 90 kilometers due east of Moscow. Vladimir is the seat of the Orthodox Church of Russia. I've often told people I had dinner with the head of the Russian Church and the Greek Orthodox Church, even though

I'm a Methodist who didn't even know who the pastor was in my own church.

I operated entirely on the come, and the class went on about two years. I gave lectures and also set the faculty up with lecturers who were really the creme-de-la-creme from Silicon Valley. That was my modus operandi throughout the whole thing.

Unfortunately, it was just a disaster. We had all the money we wanted because they would fund whatever I needed. That was never an issue. The problem was that the students were just not the right students. These kids were picked by the Communist party and their English was Russian English. I'm a very emotional guy and I like to get the students revved up. I've been that way all my life. But mid-level government bureaucrats do not have the same drive, or sometimes intelligence, as budding entrepreneurs from the free world. The material was just not going to translate, and so I told the Russians it just wasn't working. Despite being very disappointed in it, I still found it an interesting program, particularly given the context.

Throughout my time in Russia I found myself in a whole host of interesting adventures. For instance, I got to see some of the economic structure first-hand when I toured some Russian plants, though I wouldn't go inside them. They were just too dangerous to even walk on the floor. Dirty, greasy, filthy plants. Another time I got a call from a general who invited me to go for a ride in a Mig 29! That was two planes away developmentally from where they were. Not too many Americans have flown in a Mig. I said I'd love to, and we flew out of some secret service base outside northeast of Moscow. They gave us jumpsuits, the pilot got behind the controls and off we went. That was a very, very interesting day!

I kept getting myself into those kinds of things because I was not government. I was just an independent businessman. People knew I had formed the bank, and that it was successful. They were always asking how we did this or that. They asked lots of questions and wanted to know more. These were all good meetings, albeit somewhat superficial.

I was also in Moscow when the Berlin Wall came down. That was a very memorable moment. At that time I had an interpreter named André Dubinine, who was also KGB. André was a bright guy, a maverick like I am, and we really hit it off. He's a wonderful guy who later visited us in Menlo Park and Davis. He later left Russia for Switzerland where he runs a Russian insurance company in Berlin, Switzerland, and Moscow. He has done very well. I stayed in touch with him, but I haven't heard from him in a couple of years.

I had dinner with André at his house the night the wall came down. When he asked what I wanted to do that evening, I told him that I wanted to go to the church on the hill, which we could walk to, and then walk along the streets to my hotel in the Kremlin four miles away. I did a lot of walking then because that was my exercise.

Presenting to Eduard Shevardnadze

André said there were going to be a lot of people in the streets, and I told him that that was why I wanted to do it. And I had the most unusual experience one could ever have. It was a nippy cool evening, and I went to the church first. I think there must have been two to three million people in the streets of Moscow that night, and the joy was amazing. Everyone had a candle, and when you looked out over the hill, the whole scene was just glowing with candles. It was a huge celebration and I felt totally safe. It was just so much fun.

I met with Shultz every time before every trip to Russia and then debriefed with him again after I got back. I wasn't shy about letting people know I was talking to Shultz because it opened doors. For instance, he opened a door for me with a guy by the name of Jim Garrison, who was an independent politico whose principal function was to improve relationships between Russian communism and American democracy.

A short, skinny guy, Jim was really very creative and gutsy. A lot of people disliked him, but he was a very effective organizer. Jim was helpful to me, but I told Jim that even though I was an officially approved emissary, I was still a private citizen and there were certain things I needed to do on my own.

I liked Jim, and he and his staff and I worked pretty well together. One time we did so was after Brezchnev died and then-Vice President Bush went over to attend the funeral. Bush met Gorbachev and came back and told Reagan, "We can work with this guy," meaning Gorbachev. The message was that Gorbachev was a wonderful guy, so a meeting was arranged between the leaders.

At the same time, Garrison and I and others arranged a visit from Gorbachev under the auspices of The World Business Academy, which was sort of a new age group with which I was involved. The WBA had formed in San Mateo County and consisted of people that

WORLD·BUSINESS·ACADEMY
leading the way

Beyond Business —
Through Business

*Brochure for the World
Business Academy*

were really Russian and Georgian. Jim Garrison and I therefore piggybacked with the World Business Academy event onto Gorbachev's official political trip so that Gorbachev would do his Washington thing and then come speak to the World Business Academy.

Unfortunately, Garrison and I eventually split a little bit because I had the stamp of authority behind me with Shultz in a way he didn't, and because I had much sought-after expertise in business and banking that generated attention that didn't benefit him.

Gorbachev provided fresh air by opening Russia up. That guy was, I think, a political genius, and in the early 1990s, during the latter part of my involvement there, he formed a board of advisors to bounce ideas off. He was also getting money into a foundation he had set up, and he wanted a board to manage that foundation. He asked me to join, along with people like Alan Cranston, a big, tall, gaunt democratic senator and educator from California. (Even though he was too liberal for me, I really liked him.) A lot of people were very jealous of me getting that appointment, but Shultz thought it was a great idea.

The board had meetings in the Kremlin and in the U.S., and it was really fun. I was still in mid-career, with a good career behind me and a lot of successful ventures. Still, I was a bit taken back by it all…it was pretty heady stuff. I probably became a little bit arrogant, but I really thought this was going to be beneficial to the United States.

Simultaneously with all this, elections were going on in Russia. Gorbachev had released the control over all the satellite countries, like the Ukraine and Georgia. It was, basically the breakup of the USSR and I was there as that was happening too. Gorbachev was loved and hated. Apparatchiks hated him because he was completely eroding their power. The whole experience in Russia was interesting. Despite being disappointed with the classes, I had fun there and learned a great deal.

Georgia

In meeting with Gorbachev and working on his board, I became good friends with Eduard Shevardnadze, Gorbachev's secretary of state and right-hand man. During the 1986 talks in Reykjavik, Iceland, Reagan and Shultz met with Gorbachev and Shevardnadze and that foursome all became good friends politically and economically. In particular, Shevardnadze and Shultz had been opposite numbers, so Shultz was again well-positioned to weigh in on any involvement I had with Shevardnadze, who returned to his native Georgia after the breakup of the Soviet Union.

As I grew increasingly dissatisfied with the teaching program, I decided I was through working in Russia and resigned from Gorbachev's board. Shevardnadze, though, said to me, "I want you to do in Georgia what you were trying to do in Russia. We'll back you if you do it down here." Shultz was very much in favor, so I decided to go with my instincts and transition the program from Russia to Georgia. I didn't even fly through Moscow anymore. I would go to Frankfurt and then on to Tbilisi.

Georgia is a very open country…a wonderful country…and a tourist spot for the Soviet Union in the south on the Mediterranean. There are a lot of farms, and very smart people with the highest educational level in the former Soviet Union After the breakup, there was an election, and a guy by the name of Zviad Gamsakhurdia was democratically elected president. Unfortunately, he was pretty arrogant and a fascist. He had an anti-Jewish, anti-American, anti-Russian perspective and a "Georgia for Georgians" platform.

I had already decided that if I ever taught again, I was going to pick my own students and that I would require them to speak good English. I had met and befriended two Georgians, Constantine Rishnishville and Gia Bazgadze, at an art exhibit in Tbilisi, and they spoke perfect English. I told them what I was doing and that I needed them to help me select students. They agreed because we were friends and because they felt they could help Georgia.

Because Georgia was newly out from under the Russian shadow and hence as American-oriented as you can get (except for the new president), this was a time when everybody was trying to make money. Consequently, when I started the courses, people thought it was a great opportunity to get involved with an American…that they would learn something and make some connections, so it was good all the way around. The Georgians were lovely people and I felt so much at home.

With Shevardnadze's backing and Constantine and Gia's help finding a lot of really good students, I set up this class and it was beautiful. Constantine and Gia and I interviewed about 100 students, and we accepted about 30.

The incentive for the 30 in the class was that I was going to take the top half, 15, and finish the teaching over in America. I got companies to take them on as interns for about four months and to pay for their way over. I placed these students in Silicon Valley Bank, Smith Barney, lots of places. Some were married and brought their families over. This was my vision, and it had been impossible with the Russian apparatchiks. No one wanted college kids and young professionals who just wanted to take the time off to learn about what was going on in the world. but this group was bright, motivated and hard-working. They also were really motivated because of the incentives we built into the program. I only had one disappointment the entire time.

The class was roughly modern business practices, and we ran all day for two straight weeks. I would go over for that two-week period, and it was a full-time job during those two weeks because it was an intense full immersion business school course. I taught all over Georgia, but principally in Tbilisi for about five years. We used a local school and I had guys like my good friend David Elliot, who ran the largest Peace Corps program ever assembled in India, serve as visiting lecturers.

We didn't charge these students a single thing. It was gratis. I got money from the state department to help. It was a really good program, and unlike the Russian version, it was highly successful. Some of them ended up settling in California, and one of my students went back and became president of Georgia.

Wente Wines

While I was in Georgia, I got involved in the wine business. Eric Wente, a fellow Stanford grad and head of Wente Brothers Wines of Livermore, had gotten involved doing some business over there and had heard that I was also involved in Georgia. We set up a meeting to explore some opportunities and became very good friends. I also got to know his sister, Carolyn, who runs the company today, and his wife, Arel. They're a wonderful family.

Shultz still followed my path pretty closely, so I went to him and told him that Eric Wente wanted me to get in the wine business over there. Without any further inquiry, he wrote a check of $50,000 and gave it to me, saying, "Bob, invest this in Georgia. Then reinvest the profits. I don't want to see any money come out of it. I just want you to invest in Georgia." He knew that Georgia needed help and starting businesses was a way he saw to do that. George Shultz was an amazing guy. Really bright. He was so much fun to be around.

After George invested, I hired a good friend of mine by the name of Nick Frank, and we started doing a lot of serious exploration. Nick also became a partner in this venture, and we raised money and backed a Georgian group that had a winery and a wine-making equipment, so the idea was that Wente was going to teach them modern day wine practices and we would provide them the capital to work with. Eric felt they really knew what they were doing.

Unfortunately, we had problems with everything. It was the old joke: Do you know how you make a good investment in Georgia? Start with a great investment in Georgia. We got the winery going and we had vineyards out there and we bought grapes from those vineyards to process at the winery. This was a foreign product for me, but a lot of fun. People would ask me what I was doing, and I would say, "I'm investing in wine in Georgia."

Invariably the reply was, "You are *what?*"

Helga went crazy, but we got involved in everything. And we were really treated well. Georgians are great with hospitality. And I loved going there. They had been servicing as the chief tourist place for the Russians forever, so they were natural hosts. But disasters do hit.

The problem was the bottles. The bottles that were made in Georgia were just terribly inferior. The glass was bad and the seals were bad, so we bought bottles in Latvia and Lithuania. We finally heard they were on the rail coming down, but we kept waiting and waiting for them and they never came. Thousands and thousands of bottles, which we had already paid for.

At that point Constantine, Gia and I got a visa to go into Chechnya, which was where we last heard the bottles had been. Chechnya was democratic, but not exactly a friendly place. It was therefore with some fear and trepidation, which I never shared with my wife, that I went with these guys to Grozny, the capital of Chechnya.

We arrived at the railroad station, and the superintendent said, "Yeah, I think I've got your bottles." So he got in his little putt-putt, Russian-made car and we went out to a distant area of the railroad track. And there the ground is just covered with broken glass. He said, "There's your bottles!"

Who knows what happened, but obviously that was it. I guess we made a bad investment. That was the start of a lot of financial problems for the winery.

All these things have a humorous side to them, and it's just hugely entertaining, as I reminisce on how I feel about them. When I say we lost a lot of money, I lost $100,000 in there and Shultz $50,000, my friend Jim Gibbons $50,000, and about three other professors $50,000 each. All of them knew it was a high-risk thing. We were dealing in a foreign country, but we had people. Eric Wente is a good businessman. I'm a good businessman. We had good Georgian people. And we really monitored that thing, but disasters happen.

The nail in the coffin came with a guy named Nodar, who was the principal partner in the winery. He was really the guy we had invested in. Nodar had two sons, one of whom was coming home one day from the airport after picking up a buddy who was apparently on the hit list for the Georgian mafia. Both of them were murdered on the way home from the airport. Poor Nodar just went crazy. He lost his youngest son. We went to the services and Nodar cried at the wake. We went to see Nodar that night, but he had already gone. It turns out that he had he taken his revolver out to his son's grave and blown his brains out.

That really upset me. I had gotten to know him, I loved him, and he was a good guy. And I can understand; if my son was killed by the mafia, I don't know what I'd do. So that was the saga of the winery. The thing was hexed from the beginning. Both Eric and I lost a lot of money over there.

I invested in other things, like a clothing store, but the big thing I was doing was consulting with Georgian companies. I was consulting, teaching classes and investing in businesses. It was fun, and I really loved it.

The Banking System

Over time I backed off a little bit from teaching and passed it on to the local people more.

I stayed in pretty close proximity with Shevardnadze during this whole time. He became president in 1992 and then got knocked out in an election by a new kid on the street, Mikheil Saakashvili, who was a good guy and very smart. Early on banking in Georgia was largely handled by money changers on the street, maybe 90 or 100 throughout Georgia. It was what you would imagine from this kind of system: payday lending. I told Shevardnadze and Saakashvili that as a country of five million people they really needed to install a much better system, a national bank.

I worked with the two of them on it and brought in Price Waterhouse and developed a strategic plan for the establishment of the new banking system for the whole country. They established a national bank and got it organized under the auspices of the federal government. That really went well. It was fun to do. I really feel very proud about that. It is still functioning just as we set it up and a lot of those practices and procedures are still in effect.

Tying Things up

I had been going to eastern Europe maybe 20 times a year for a couple weeks at a time. So I spent a lot of time there. I stayed in private homes to save money, and I got to know the people and got involved in those people's affairs.

Near the end of my time over there, a guy named Mike Clayton came into the picture. Mike was with a USAID program, establishing a better corporate structure for small towns in outlying communities. He had started over there right after I started. Mike was a Stanford guy who had gone to business school on the east coast. He was 20 years younger than me, and we worked a lot together over there trying to start a couple of businesses.

Mike had a relationship with a young Georgian named Sasha who was in Shevardnadze's cabinet, doing very well and we really liked him. He was also very active in the Greens Party. My son Dale was a German Green and he worked with the head people in the German Greens.

Helga did two trips with me because she missed me being gone. I also took Dale to Georgia and introduced him to my friends there. Dale always said "Dad, you ought to meet these German guys," so he would bring them down to Georgia. It was really fun working with Dale and with all of these men who were his friends, and we had some interesting experiences.

On one of our trips there was shooting going on in the streets. It was about 2 o'clock in the morning and we'd just arrived. We were sitting there having a drink and this guy walked in drunk as a skunk and carrying an oozi and an AK-47. He was bleeding like mad from bandage around his head. How he got through security I'll never know.

I said, "Dale, let's get out of here. Let's go up to the room and lock the door." We got in the elevator, and it was one of these glass elevators. We could see the guy down there starting to look up and for him it would have been a perfect turkey shoot. We were completely trapped and exposed.

Dale agreed. "Let's get out of the Metechi Hotel. You brought me six thousand miles to die in the lobby of the Metechi! What kind of father are you?" Dale always had this little wrinkle with partial truth and partial arrogance. He is a master at it.

Sasha was a wonderful guy, very popular and we hoped he might be president. I thought he was going to be. Then, one time while we were there, he was murdered by the mafia from Armenia operating probably on behalf of a political opponent. That was just a tragic to me because I liked the guy so well. Very candidly, after his death I lost interest. There had been multiple deaths and business successes and business failures, and I was pretty much done with it all. This was in 2006, and it had been almost 20 years since I had started in Russia.

Helga and I decided to move to Davis, where I had a lot of friends and some opportunities and the university, so that was clearly going to be the next stage of our lives.

Chapter Nine:
A New Life in Davis

The traffic was getting worse and worse in Palo Alto, so we bought the house in Davis on Miller Drive in 1989 as a weekend place.

I taught at Stanford throughout the nineties, and it was during this time that the dean of the School of Management at Davis, Bob Smiley, who knew of me through friends of his. He asked me if I'd teach a course there. I ended up teaching a similar course to the one I had been teaching at Stanford, but the students were a lot different at Davis, so I had to feel my way through that. But it was still based on my experiences in Georgia. We also brought Georgian students over and put them in school at Davis, and that worked really well. That's also where I picked up guys like Steven Lease, who was one of my students. Steven later joined Morgan Stanley and is now my financial adviser. Steven's a very brainy guy and wonderful to work with.

I wanted to continue serving on boards, and Bob put me on the Dean's Advisory Board for the Graduate School of Management, which is how I got involved in the building drive. There was no fee on that one. I also served six years on the University of California at Davis Development Board, which is like an endowment board at Stanford. We managed their contributions. There were a lot of good men and women on these boards, and it was rewarding to have a good connection with UC Davis, but I said I didn't want to serve any more than one term. But that's how I got involved at UC Davis and it was all great. I loved it, and those things set the foundation for the final phases of my life.

Helga and I finally moved to Davis full time in about 2000. I had been teaching at Stanford for 31 years, and I just decided at that point I wasn't going to do it anymore. I didn't want to make the long trips back to Palo Alto after we moved to Davis; I was winding down. The more I became engaged at Davis, the less I was involved at Stanford. I

With Helga, the love of my life

also switched my giving to Davis because I was involved with the community and it helped me integrate into the city. The only thing I do at Stanford now involves fundraising for the Clark Oglesby Fund which I had set up in the 70s.

We were very happy and engaged in our new community, and now I'm planted here, retired here. Ilsi's here and she is very accomplished in what she loves, which is to be an active veterinarian in the Winters to Santa Rosa area. In 2010, I finally backed off the teaching at Davis, but I still served on a lot of committees. My thrust was to try to contribute to this university, which has the world's leading agricultural veterinary schools—two leading schools in the world wrapped up in one institution.

I think what Stanford did is directly applicable to what is going on at Davis in terms of technology. At Davis we need to learn how to free the technology and get it in the hands of the doers and the thinkers, the people who can use it. We also need to establish relationships with major funders. Frederick Terman, Stanford's former dean of engineering when I was a student, did that at Stanford, and then the next three or four deans and presidents followed suit. John Hennessy was the latest one. He went out and developed a company and made significant amount of money and came back in and became president of Stanford. He also gave a lot of money to the University. Stanford now has alumni and friends who have given hundreds of millions of dollars. How many schools can say that? I don't think there is another one.

Now, there is a lot of difference between Davis and Stanford. There is really no comparison, so my focus was how to get more technology out of the institution and into the marketplace. The comparison is trying to get the faculty oriented in a different line of thinking, but it's really hard to do. My friend Andy Hargadon is a professor of management at Davis, and his specialties are entrepreneurship and enterprise development. He and his wife have been leading forces in this effort. I knew Andy's father when he was dean of admissions at Stanford, and his wife, Annie, worked at hospice, so she knew Helga, who volunteered there as well. I've now worked over the years with Andy trying to build up technology and entrepreneurship at Davis. We have made slow but steady progress.

I really got wrapped up in the agriculture. Davis has a sustainability program out on West Russell toward Winters, run by Professor Tom Tomich, along with Jim Hill and Bruce Hammock. They are all botanists and biochemists and good people.

Companies

When I got started at Davis I was still on a few boards, and it was a lot of fun and very rewarding. I had ended up being chairman of some of them, except the foundation board. The whole thing really started with Silicon Valley Bank. I had left there, but I was still at GeoEx, and there were two others that were significant in which I became involved.

The first was Solaicx. In about 2001, an entrepreneur named Tom Ford asked if I would join him in developing a better silicon wafer. He knew I had had experience with solar cells through working with my dear friend Jim Gibbons. Jim and I went way back; we had been in a book group and played tennis together. Professionally, Jim was the head of Stanford's electrical engineering department and later dean of engineering. He had developed Stanford's semiconductor fabrication lab, and hence was essentially one of the founding fathers of Silicon Valley. He also had a little company called Solar Energy Research Associates (SERA). Jim was a mentor to me, and we talked a lot about solar energy, so he was my source of energy and inspiration on this matter.

The specific role of the silicon wafer is to allow a solar cell to convert photons, which are the form in which the light from the sun hits the cell, freeing these electrons to be captured as energy.

Solaics wafers power solar cells like these throughout the country

The key is to grab that photon quickly, because if it doesn't get converted into electrons, it just dissipates. The photovoltaic panel then takes the electrons and pumps it out as energy. The point is maximum conversion for maximum energy.

Ford was a young man, and he and his team of four guys had a pretty good idea how to develop a crystal growth manufacturing technology to produce low-cost, high-efficiency monocrystalline silicon wafers to maximize efficiency and energy output. I listened to them, and I said, "I like your idea," so in about 2001 we started Solaicx.

I used to go down to Solaicx's offices in San Jose because I could commute by rail. I got off at '49er stadium and the office was a block and a half away....so I would just walk over from the railroad station. I was particularly close to two other people on the board. One was the son of Chuck Schwab and the other was Alex

Wong, a senior executive with D.E. Shah. Alex was wonderful, a very bright man. He was in charge of their entrepreneurial activities.

By about 2007 Silicon Valley had become a very expensive place. The employees had to buy expensive homes, not by intent, but because they had to live there. Everything drove everything else up. It was just unbelievable. We were also expending huge amounts of power to make these wafers in California.

We found producing things in Portland to be less costly because of the availability of cheap Columbia River power, so we moved the plant there. I then went up there at least once a month, when we had our board meetings, and sometimes more often than that. We brought a lot of capital into the firm, and I was involved in hiring. We had brilliant people— chemical engineers and so on. I was with them until we sold the company to MEMC Electronic Materials Inc. in 2010. I had been chairman the whole ten years. It was a wonderful company for me to be involved in.

Engage3 was the last of the companies I've been involved with since coming to Davis. Engage3 has algorithms and programs that assist supermarkets and supply stores and other types of business more effectively price their goods by using data science and artificial intelligence-powered software. This allows them to be more competitive in their pricing and to have inventory control as well as cost control all in one evaluation package. It's unique.

Brothers Ken and Tim Ouimet are the owners of Engage3. Ken is a graduate of the University of California-Davis, and we're good friends. For instance, he once gave me a book on conversations with God, which I found really interesting. He just wanted to discuss it with me. We would do things like that with each other.

One brother went to school and one didn't. You can't tell the difference in brilliance. Ken's a little bit more polished maybe but that's about it. They had begun by working with their father in the grocery business and then developed these pricing algorithms.

Ken came to me one day, and said, "Bob, I need someone to give me some sound advice." When Ken told me what he was doing, I thought it was very intriguing. He had laid a lot of it down on paper, but it was still an idea. The more I got thinking about it, the more intriguing it seemed, and I told him he ought to do it. That's how I arrive at a lot of these things. Gut instinct.

Ken was forming a board, but I told him I didn't think I should be on the board, but I ended up sitting in on all the board meetings. I'm just an adviser to the board, so I have absolutely no axe to grind and can tell him the way I think it is. He loves it. I was well paid between cash and stock, I don't need the money, but I like to be paid, because when people pay, they use your knowledge. If they didn't pay me anything, they wouldn't pay any attention to what I was saying.

Engage3 raised some money, and they now have 38+ employees and are in an office building on the corner of Second and D Street in Davis. Another start-up here in town was producing electronics, and at one point they had their production plant in Belgium! I told them that they didn't have any control over it. If they didn't speak Belgian, how were they going to manage it? So I told Ken to put that engineering right in the same building where they could walk through the office daily. It was the biggest and best change they ever made.

Common Sense. That is what business is.... common sense. People don't recognize it, because too few people use common sense. I feel this is my forte.

I like Ken Ouimet. He's brilliant. I like where they're located, so I've worked with him and with every senior management person at Engage3. I'm still very involved with the company. And I'm also still doing GeoEx. So those are the two companies I have left. I get insignificant fees out of both, I don't charge them hardly anything, and I'm not doing that much for them. If I got involved again, I would raise my fees. Every once in a while, those things kick in and you sell, and you make money. It takes every ounce of energy I have but I need to do it. I'll continue attending the board meetings, but because of my age I don't think I'll be adding much anymore.

Health Problems

My lifelong friend Gordon Smith and I both had major health issues in one year, about 2016. Gordon came home one day and got to his driveway and said, "What do I do now?" He didn't know what to do. Helen, his wife, came down and they got him to the hospital. He had had a stroke. That pretty well ended his career.

About the same time, I had what I then thought was my first, silent heart attack. I was out at Russell Ranch with Rochelle Swanson, who was a city council woman, and we were working on some University of California-Davis business. At one point I said, "Rochelle, I'm not feeling well." I went and laid down on the seat of her Suburban and fell asleep, then woke up feeling pretty good. I had arranged for lunch over at Putah Creek Cafe in Winters, but I asked Rochelle to drive me home. Helga took me right over to the hospital. They did all sorts of tests on me and said I had had a fairly sizable silent heart attack.

Subsequently, Ilsi and I figured out that it had happened about four months earlier when Dale's kids were out. We had taken a hike up in the Sierras, just off of I-80. We were up above Salmon Lake, and I didn't feel really well that time either. I'm not a climber, but I'm a good hiker. I've been up to 20,500 feet without oxygen, but that day I was just too exhausted to hike, so I laid down and took a nap and felt a lot better. I got up walked back, and we then had a great party coming in at a place up in Woodland. All the family was out, and it was a wonderful time.

I was troubled by the whole thing and recognized that there was something major going on with me. The end result of that was that I had a series of heart attacks from that point. Helga and I talked a lot about it. One thing led to another. I had all the MRIs and so on and I felt better but no major work was done on my heart at that point.

Helga's Death

The next year, 2017, my brother and a lot of family members had come up for my birthday on the 18th of May, but the celebration was suspended after Helga's sudden death. We had a great time except for one thing: my wife was no longer there. We went ahead and had the birthday celebration, but this has been the single most difficult part in life. I'm still not over it. She was one wonderful woman.

Helga died on May 16. She was in the process of healing from a broken hip and had been home almost a week that morning. That day was so typical! We got up and I made breakfast. I picked her clothes out, bathed her, dressed her. She was in great health and happy. We talked.

We'd get through that each morning and I'd go back out and make a phone call or two. Then we'd talk a little bit more about things. That morning she said she'd the nicest call with Ilsi and three other friends had called.

Then all of a sudden, she was gone. She just passed. I later learned that this happens a lot to women in their eighties after hip surgery. I was a broken man for a while. I'm rallying now but it's been very, very difficult. For instance, the church service last night played *Be Now My Vision*, which is a song that Helga and I both loved. I break up every time I hear it. I miss that woman so much.

I still have her ashes in the next room. When my time comes, I want to mix our ashes together and spread them at some mountain peak. Ken will do it, and however he does it, his choice will be fine with Helga and me.

The Last Heart Attack

The year after Helga passed, 2018, and shortly before I sold the house on Miller Drive and moved into URC, I had another heart attack.

Ilsi had been my principal care provider in recent years, and I had wanted to take her and Clare to Alaska. We were going to take a small boat up the Inland Passage and kayak, but a few days before we were to leave, once again I didn't feel good. It felt like the good Lord was telling me to get to the hospital.

I went to my physician, Steve Smith, and they ran a quick test on me and determined that I needed to be in cardiac care immediately. I went by ambulance over to Sacramento where they did nine days of work on my heart. I had another heart attack while I was there, and they put in three stents through two arteries, one from the right leg one and from the left leg. Those worked wonders.

Because this was after Helga's death, the truth is that I really didn't want to come home. I was ready to just hang it up. I really tried to will myself to die. But when I woke up that morning, I felt better than I had felt in 10 years. It was the stents: they were getting more oxygen to the heart – 99% oxygen flow.

I've had no incidents since then and I've been home ever since. Three years after Helga's death I've been able to pick up and go on to some extent, which she would have wanted me to do. I was dating a lady in San Francisco, but I met a wonderful woman named Ann Corley here at the University Retirement Center, and we spend a lot of time together. I know Helga would approve. We had talked about this kind of thing. Ann was a Presbyterian minister, and her husband was in business, but he passed at URC. I still miss Helga and I'm sure Ann misses her husband, but we enjoy each other's company. I am blessed to have such a warm and loving woman in my life. We were going to go to Europe earlier this year before the pandemic hit. Minor health challenges pop up for both of us, but we are relatively healthy and we're very lucky to be able to have each other.

I'm feeling pretty good now for 89 years old. People comment that I look good. I think I'm healthy, and my mind is pretty sharp. I still enjoy the involvement I have with GeoEx and Engage3. I still enjoy my friends. My M.O. now is new conversations and thoughts. I miss Helga desperately, but there's a lot to be thankful for with Ann and Ilsi looking after me, and the boys and their families coming out when they can.

I'm grateful.

RWM

Epilogue

From a business standpoint, was I successful? There really is no right answer and no wrong answer. At one point, after Silicon Valley Bank and a couple of the other successful start-ups, some people thought Medearis had a magic wand. That's nuts. I didn't have a magic wand...but I didn't mind people thinking I did. If I succeeded, it was because of hard work, a knack for picking the right people, and relatively good judgement. My instincts were good, and I listened to them. Sometimes it's luck as much as anything else, and I was always pretty lucky, which never hurts. As a result of all that, people had confidence in me.

To be honest, I had some wins and a few losses, which isn't bad. If you bat 50/50 as an entrepreneur, you're way ahead of the game. The ratio of successes in venture capital is maybe one in fifteen.

I started in real estate, of course, toyed with government work, and taught at Stanford and Davis for over 30 years. What I liked most, though, was being an idea guy, an entrepreneur and a board member. The fact is I like to be my own boss. And once I got something up and running, I had no interest in managing it, but I was always happy to continue to consult either as a board member or as an unofficial adviser. I also didn't work well with people I did not respect or that I didn't think capable when I could find others who were more capable. It's not surprising, then, that most of my successes have been start-ups of one kind or another, and in working with people I liked and respected. Along the way, I learned a lot of lessons.

Generally, for a startup to be successful, it's better if it's developed by the person who had the idea in the first place. Robert Noyce had a great idea at Intel: he developed it and it was an immediate success. That doesn't sound difficult, but it is, and boy, is it important. Noyce executed on it and proved his idea in the marketplace. That's the final judgement on whether your idea is good.

For me, the question became, "What does it take to get this idea from an idea from paper into reality?" It's not an easy thing to do. I would just sit down and play around with starting a plan, like I did with the bank, or with Haresh Shah at Risk Management, because I recognized a good idea when I saw one. And I literally mean "play" with it.... what if we did this or that? Look at it from all sides. Some of these venture capitalists are very good at playing with ideas, examining it this way and then that way.

Silicon Valley Bank was started on the premise that we could provide needed second-round funding to entrepreneurs that wasn't provided by the venture community. At the bank we did a few things that were pretty unusual, like getting the venture capitalists to buy in, and on our timetable. This was the only requirement of the VC's: to provide equity capital. I just told them I wanted their deposits in my bank, which was not a hard thing to ask for because they had high amounts of money and so they were going to have big deposits. All I was doing was asking for a disproportionate share for the risk that they were taking. Up until that time, banks hadn't operated in markets that were chaotic and volatile, but we did it.

Whatever the idea or approach, one of the first rules of successful implementation involves putting the right people in the right jobs and giving them a sense of belonging. I had pretty solid people selection skills, and consequently, I made my biggest mistakes when I didn't follow my instincts. For instance, once or twice I knew someone was the wrong person for the job, but I didn't have the guts to say it, because he was a good friend, and I didn't want to hurt his feelings. That happened at the bank. I wanted to get a particular person in as chief financial officer, but they hired someone else, and I think they were probably right. It was one of the best hiring decisions the bank ever made. So yeah, I've made some mistakes.

My greatest frustrations in start-ups involved people who may have been absolutely geniuses in terms of their idea but were not the right people to run the company. Another frustration involved a failure to take the first step. I've seen people in the academic profession that had the greatest ideas in the world, but they were afraid of taking that first step. It's hard for some people, and you have to be sensitive to that.

Timing is another critical factor. I would say that very often some of the worst decisions people make are around timing. Would IBM be as successful if it had been tried in 1938? No, because they didn't have the supporting cast to do anything. Timing is everything.

Cash flow is yet another major factor. Nothing is as important as adequate cash flow; too little is another big source of failure. Unfortunately, many people don't pay enough attention to it.

Many people wanted to start something, asked my advice, and then asked if I would be interested in investing. With all of the above in mind, I'd say, "Not on your life…at least until I know what the start-up is. I want to see it in paper. I want to see it written down. I want to know who's involved. I want to understand the timing. I want to see the projected cash flow."

As the businessperson on the team, you have to weigh all of this to understand where something is headed. The beginning of Risk Management Solutions (RMS) was a good example. Professor Haresh Shah had the idea. He hired a PhD who cultivated and developed the idea. Then I got involved and we figured out how to structure that company so that it was going to do the job that it needed to do, and to get the revenue that it needed to be successful. I am proud to have helped start that company because, even though they had a good idea, they didn't know how to put the team together.

Again, so much of it is just taking the first step. Then there is a certain progression in the decision-making process that gets you from idea to a business practice to a business plan to execution to getting the money. It's a whole series of things, but it's not a set critical path in which you proceed precisely 1-2-3-4 in all circumstances. It might be 1-4-2-3-9-7, or any other series of steps. At some point, though, there is some magic formula, a particular road, or if you're lucky, a couple of roads to success. I go back to a quote from Robert Frost who wrote about "the road less traveled." In start-ups you often have to find the less traveled road to be successful. The point is, there is no standard formula as to how you get started and proceed.

From a best practices perspective, the fundamental problem when you do a start-up is that each one is different. The lessons learned from one may in some instances apply to others, but usually not all of them, and certainly not always. People are always looking for the magic formula. As I've outlined, some of the common factors are the quality of the idea, the timing, the inculcation of the data into the process, cash flow, the timing and the people that are necessary to get it from A to B. Right people. Right job. Right time. Enough cash. Thousands of things. But here's the real magic: hard work and stick-to-it-iviness.

Underlying Principles

Strategies for success are one thing, but you need to have an underlying set of principles or philosophies. An approach to business. The guy that taught me the most about that was Professor Dorio at Harvard. For instance, one of his things was being on time. If people weren't there at 8:00 for an 8:00 class, he'd literally lock the late students out of the room. If they couldn't be on time, he didn't want them in class. He called it "Dorio time", which is five minutes ahead of the actual time. This is something I practiced all my life. Of course, it drives me nuts when I'm the one who is late, and I profusely apologize. I set my own watch ahead, and I expect people to be on time.

At the same time, you can't be rigid. I think it's bad judgement to walk out on a meeting you're waiting for if they are 15 minutes late, because there could be a thousand reasons why they might be late. You have to have sympathy and understanding and see what the reason is. Always look for the unexpected. You get to someone's office and he's late, but you shouldn't get upset before you have all the data, because that's when you find out his wife has just committed suicide, or he was in a car accident.

In short, you have to be understanding when things happen to others. You have to be very forgiving. My wife was such a wonderful teacher in that area. There were times when I was sort of arrogant. It's not my nature, and I didn't mean to be, but at times I was, and Helga would just slap me down beautifully. She was just that kind of person. What a beautiful teacher she was. Just unbelievable!

You also have to realize that you will never get all the information you need. At some point you have to recognize there is a time to make a decision. That's a tough one to teach young people who are learning to make decisions and want more and more information. The fact is that very often you're just not going to have all the information you'd like, or you think you need when it comes time to make the decision. You have to go ahead and make it with the information you have.

The biggest weakness that I've always had is paying attention. If you are focused on something else, you don't hear the data that is being presented to you. I was often guilty of that. It happened to me a lot. I'd be sitting there and thinking about one thing and then get off on another track and lose my whole focus. When you are doing start-ups, you really can't afford to do that.

I don't have a whole lot of regrets. I wish I would have been a better student. I don't think I learned as much as I could have learned. I always felt people knew a lot more than I did…and I think I'm right on that! I'll also never forget going to Harvard and running into WACs— Written Analysis of Cases. I'm not a good writer, so they were challenging. The fact that I don't write well has always bugged me, and I always regretted not focusing more on English. I'm a very good speaker, though, and that has served me well.

"IF YOUR ACTIONS INSPIRE OTHERS TO DREAM MORE, LEARN MORE, DO MORE AND BECOME MORE, YOU ARE A LEADER."
-John Quincy Adams

ROBERT MEDEARIS IS SUCH A PERSON

Founding member of numerous institutions, pioneer in the creation of electronic industries, and investor in new enterprises. Bob advised leaders of the Republic of Georgia and officials of the U.S. Government. He was a consulting professor to Stanford University (emeritus) and taught at UC Davis Graduate School of Business. Bob holds concerns for our nation and its humanity while holding sacred his family love and pride of rural heritage.

Presented to Bob on the occasion of his commemoration on November 30, 2017 at Stanford University by his close friends Dr. Leon and Nina Garoyan.

As you approach retirement you sit back and reflect on what you did. That's why one of the most meaningful things that ever happened was a dinner in my honor at Stanford on November 20, at which I was honored after 31 years of teaching in the engineering department and starting several companies. But it was a very nice thing, and I was proud to be honored. My only regret was that the dinner was in November of 2017 and that Helga had died in May of that year.

I didn't bat 1,000, but nobody does. I mentored a lot of students at Stanford, and also from Georgia. I helped people start a bunch of really good companies, and the bank which still is a driver in Silicon Valley. I had good mentors and a lot of help. I learned a lot and had fun bringing ideas to fruition in several different fields or helping others do so. I think I made a variety of contributions and helped more than a few people, and I'm happy about that.

What Really Matters

I really enjoyed teaching at Stanford and teaching in Georgia and at Davis, and some of my students even became business partners and advisers. Raising your own kids and grandkids is of course the most important and the most rewarding. I'm deeply proud of all my three children and my four grandchildren. I'm no longer teaching but I get to mentor the grandkids sometimes.

The entire family at Yellowstone National Park. Top row, left to right, Ken, Rob, Sarah, Dale, Amy, Ilsi, Clare, Helga and Bob. Bottom row, Dale and Amy's daughters, Tori, Mia, and Eliza

For instance, Ken's son, Rob, and I will go fishing and little things will start to come out. "Grandpa," he said one time, "I really want to go into the service." Which we discussed and which he did. I've always approached these situations indirectly. The worst thing I can do is ask the obvious question and grill them head on. But if we go fishing...we can see what comes up in passing. It's like playing with the fish. A tug or the nibble starts and then you pull on it a bit and you can hook 'em. Then the excitement of really fishing—or talking heart to heart— comes. But I've had to learn to listen, learn to be intuitive. And in general, I've learned that indirect teaching is the best way to do it, particularly with your own kids and

Fishing with my grandson, Rob

grandchildren. Fortunately, I've become pretty good at cutting to the chase, but indirectly.

Helga and I were blessed with each of our children and grandchildren. I'm not only proud of them, and have enjoyed their various successes, I love them. Ken and Dale and Ilsi have been there for me as I've moved into retirement, and Ilsi in particular has been my steadfast caregiver and advocate here in northern California.

The seminal moment of my entire life clearly occurred at the history corner of Stanford's quad at 11:55 on March 8th, 1953. That's where I met Helga Biermer, in the archway at the top of the steps. I saw this girl and she was just as gorgeous as she was in the *Chapparal Magazine* where I'd first seen her picture. It was game, set and match in 30 seconds. Helga was not only brilliant – she is

Helga and I with our grown children

fluent in Spanish, English and German, and speaks without an accent, and she could probably get by in French—but she was a wonderful, brilliant nurse who earned her doctorate and an incredibly giving soul who all her life gave unceasingly to others and to her family and to me. For me she was a marvelous traveling companion on our many trips and throughout life. She taught me so much. I can't say enough things about my wife...I can't believe she's gone. I have nothing but loving memories of her existence and I miss her terribly every day. A finer woman never walked the earth.

I sold our house on Miller Drive in Davis in 2018 and moved into a single apartment at the University Retirement Community a couple of miles away. I still serve on a couple of boards and try to stay busy seeing friends. I'm pretty healthy, currently recovering from a broken hip, and blessed to see Ilsi and Clare on a regular basis. I look forward to seeing Kenny and Dale and their families again when the current pandemic subsides.

I continue to be blessed by the loving companionship of Ann Corley. She has meant so much to me as a loving companion over these last couple of years.

I love her deeply and she has made my life so much more wonderful.

I'm in no hurry to move on, but when I do, I'll be ready. For now, I'm surrounded by Ann and family and friends. I enjoy this companionship in my final days and I'm able to look back on a wonderful life. I hope I earned it, but I also realize that, as with business, sometimes you get lucky. I certainly did.

RWM

Addendum to Chapter One

Official History of Lieutenant William Garner's Battery "H" of Michigan's 1st Regiment, Light Artillery ("De Golyer's Battery")

Organized at Monroe, Mich., and mustered in March 6, 1862.

Left State for St. Louis, Mo., March 13; thence moved to New Madrid, Mo. Attached to Artillery Division, Army of the Mississippi, to July, 1862. District of Columbus, Ky., Dept. of the Tennessee, to November, 1862. Artillery, 3rd Division, Right Wing 13th Army Corps (Old), Dept. of the Tennessee, to December, 1862. Artillery, 3rd Division, 17th Army Corps, Army of the Tennessee, to October, 1864. Post of Chattanooga, Tenn., Dept. of the Cumberland, October, 1864. Post of Nashville, Tenn., Dept. of the Cumberland, to February, 1865. Post of Chattanooga, Tenn., Dept. of the Cumberland, to July, 1865.

SERVICE. Operations against Island No. 10, Mississippi River, March 15-April 8, 1862. Expedition down the Mississippi River to Fort Pillow, Tenn., May 19-23. Duty in District of Columbus, Ky., until November. Expedition from Columbus, Ky., to Covington, Durhamsville and Fort Randolph September 28-October 5. Grant's Central Mississippi Campaign November 2, 1862, to January 10, 1863. Reconnaissance from Lagrange November 8-9, 1862. Moved to Memphis, Tenn., January, 1863; thence to Lake Providence, La., February 22. Duty there and at Milliken's Bend, La., until April 25. Movement on Bruinsburg and turning Grand Gulf April 25-30. Battle of Thompson's Hill, Port Gibson, Miss., May 1. South Fork, Bayou Pierrie, May 2. Forty Hills and Hankinson's Ferry May 3-4. Battles of Raymond May 12, Jackson May 14, and Champion's Hill May 16. Siege of Vicksburg, Miss., May 18-July 4. Assaults on Vicksburg May 19 and 22. Surrender of Vicksburg July 4. Duty at Vicksburg until February, 1864. Expedition to Monroe, La., August 20-September 2, 1863. Expedition to Canton October 14-20. Bogue Chitto Creek October 17. Duty at Big Black November 8, 1863, to February, 1864. Meridian Campaign February 3-March 2. Clinton February 5. Meridian February 14-15. Moved to Clifton, Tenn., April; thence march to Ackworth, Ga., May 5-June 8. Atlanta (Ga.) Campaign June 8-September 8. Operations about Marietta and against Kennesaw Mountain June 10-July 2. Assault on Kennesaw June 27. Nickajack Creek July 2-5. Howell's Ferry July 5. Chattahoochee River July 5-17. Leggett's (or Bald Hill) July 20-21. Battle of Atlanta July 22. Siege of Atlanta July 22-August 25. Flank movement on Jonesboro August 25-30. Battle of Jonesboro August 31-September 1. Lovejoy Station September 2-6. Duty near Atlanta till October. Reconnaissance from Rome, on Cave Springs Road, and skirmishes October 12-13. Guard Railroad near Chattanooga, Tenn., until November. Moved to Nashville, Tenn., November 15-18, and duty there until February, 1865. Battle of Nashville December 15-16, 1864 (Reserve). Moved to Chattanooga February 16-19, 1865, and duty there until July. Ordered to Jackson, Mich. and there mustered out July 22, 1865.

Battery lost during service 2 Officers and 3 Enlisted men killed and mortally wounded and 42 Enlisted men by disease. Total 47.

RWM

Addendum Two:
Board Memberships

- Lusk Corporation – Homebuilding
- HCC – Construction
- Silicon Valley Bank
- Wilsey & Ham – Civil Engineering
- WH Pacific – Civil Engineering
- Commerce Security Bank
- Solaics – Photovoltaic Cells
- Engage3 – Electronic Pricing Systems
- GeoEx: Exotic travel
- Opthalmic Imaging Systems
- PAMA Development – Construction
- Lytton Gardens – A Senior Housing Project
- Tucson Homebuilders Association
- Numerous non-profit corporations